RISK
MANAGEMENT

RISK
MANAGEMENT
Survival Tools for Law Firms

THIRD EDITION

Anthony E. Davis and
Katie M. Lachter

ABA**LAW**
PRACTICE
DIVISION
The Business of Practicing Law

Library of Congress Cataloging-in-Publication Data

Davis, Anthony E., 1949- author.
  Risk management : survival tools for law firms / by Anthony E. Davis and Katie M. Lachter. — Third edition.
     pages cm
  Includes bibliographical references and index.
  ISBN 978-1-62722-326-3 (print : alk. paper)
  1. Lawyers—Malpractice—United States. 2. Practice of law—United States. 3. Law firms—United States. 4. Lawyers—Malpractice—Australia—New South Wales. I. Lachter, Katie M., author. II. American Bar Association. Section of Law Practice Management. III. Title.
  KF313.D38 2015
  340.068'1—dc23

                                                                            2015027231

CONTENTS

**PART 3:   Quality/In Control (QUIC) Survey for Law Firms
Answer and Analysis (Crib) Sheets   91**

FOREWORD

In solo law practices on Main Street and transnational firms on Wall Street, lawyers' roles are changing. Rather than waiting for difficulties to arise, lawyers provide valuable assistance by helping clients avoid problems and comply with legal requirements. Over the past decade, the compliance field has grown, and law schools have expanded their programs to prepare graduates for new career opportunities.

Law schools and legal employers have devoted far less attention to preparing lawyers to comply with professional regulations related to law practice. Even less attention is devoted to training lawyers to recognize and manage risk. Although some bar associations and professional liability insurers have developed educational materials and tools, the scope and reach of these resources is limited. Thankfully, the third edition of *Risk Management: Survival Tools for Law Firms*, by Anthony E. Davis and Katie M. Lachter, does a remarkable job in filling the gap. The book can be a game changer for lawyers who want to improve their risk management efforts. It provides important context and perspective, as well as practical guidance for firm leaders and practicing lawyers.

In the first edition of the book, Anthony E. Davis gave practitioners a very useful resource to use in developing and evaluating firm policies and procedures related to risk management. The second edition refined the approach. Now, the third edition expands the coverage, homing in on many areas of concern for lawyers practicing in a heavily regulated and complex legal environment. As the authors of the third edition note, the structure and delivery of legal services has radically changed since publication of the second edition, exponentially broadening the risks that lawyers and their firms encounter. As a result, they suggest that risk management is no longer limited to avoiding malpractice claims and professional discipline, but requires an understanding of how the new universe of risk can undermine a law firm's reputation and ability to exist. With the failure of major law firms, these words should ring true with readers.

Unlike some other guides and books that provide only self-assessment checklists, *Risk Management: Survival Tools for Law Firms* first offers insights on an effective risk management program. Part 1 of the book helps readers understand the importance of risk management and the steps for implementing an effective risk management system. Chapter 1 opens with an inclusive definition of risk as "*anything* that interferes with the ability of the firm and its lawyers to provide legal services and generate a profit from doing so." If lawyers recognize that risk management goes beyond addressing malpractice and professional discipline threats, they will be more inclined to support risk management efforts.

Part 2 of the book includes self-assessment questionnaires for nine main categories for evaluating risk management, starting with a questionnaire for assessing risk issues related to the firm's management structure and continuing through to the last questionnaire dealing with non-technology-related disaster recovery planning. The separate questionnaire approach is very helpful in giving readers a road map to use in completing what otherwise would be an overwhelming process. With this approach, readers can tackle risk management as a continuous process, completing a comprehensive review a spoonful at a time.

To provide guidance on the significance of questionnaire responses, part 3 includes crib sheets for analyzing the answers and determining steps to be taken to address deficiencies revealed by the self-assessment form. In reading and following the guidance provided in the three parts of the book, readers learn about risk management on the macro level of institutional concerns and the micro level of specific systems. With respect to both levels, the authors pose a fundamental question, asking readers to seriously examine where their firms stand on issues of ethics and risk management.

In discussing the successful implementation of risk management, a number of themes emerge. From the beginning, the authors emphasize that meaningful risk management starts at the top. It is crucial for the leadership to embrace risk management, rewarding compliance efforts and dealing with noncompliance. With management support and an institutional commitment, it is more likely that firm lawyers will participate in meaningful periodic reviews.

A related theme is that effective risk management requires candor and willingness on the part of lawyers to engage in serious examination, beyond going through the motions and checking off boxes. This type of candid self-assessment can help firm leaders determine if there is a disconnect between what controls they believe are in place and what lawyers actually do in the trenches of everyday practice. As suggested, the reviews should not be mechanistic, but be part of a fluid and organized process of carefully evaluating current controls and possibilities for improvement.

Another noteworthy premise is that "one size does not fit all." Although the authors provide tools, explanations, and suggestions for adopting and implementing practice controls, they emphasize that it is incumbent on lawyers to design measures and systems that are appropriate to the risks faced by the particular lawyers, their firms, and their firm culture.

Regardless of the circumstances and culture within a particular firm or practice, the authors underscore the importance of individual responsibility and accountability. As they suggest, no one can be above risk management controls because the firm only succeeds if each lawyer is accountable for his or her own conduct.

Finally, the theme that resonated with me the most is the one that relates to the merger of good ethics and good business. By avoiding problems and improving legal services provided, law firms can be more profitable. This was a lesson that I drew from empirical studies of a new regulatory regime for incorporated firms in Australia. Chapter 2 of the book discusses the approach in the Australian state of New South Wales, which requires that incorporated law firms adopt appropriate management systems to assure compliance with standards for legal practitioners. To assist lawyers in evaluating their management systems, the regulator in New South Wales first implemented a self-assessment process, requiring that a designated person for the firm rate the firm's compliance with ten objectives of sound practice. An early empirical study revealed that the average number of complaints against firms that completed the self-assessment process went down by two-thirds after the firm completed the assessment. Another noteworthy finding was that the average complaints against the incorporated firms that completed the self-assessment process were one-third of those against firms that had not completed the assessment. Following this study of complaint rates, I completed my own empirical study on the impact of the requirement that firms implement appropriate management systems and complete a self-assessment process. Findings from my study indicated that the Australian system of requiring self-assessments successfully provides firm leaders the incentives, tools, and authority to take steps to develop management systems. Evidently, a significant percentage of directors learned from the process, taking steps to avoid problems and complaints, as evidenced by the significant reduction in the number of complaints against firms that completed the assessment. The quantitative complaints data, coupled with the findings from my study, make a compelling case for devoting time and effort to ethics audits within the firm.

Interestingly, the firms most motivated to undertake the self-assessment were those that recognized the connection between management systems, profitability and client retention. Some firm leaders have actually sought International Organization of Standardization certifications for their firms' systems in an effort to distinguish their firms in the marketplace.

In studying the self-assessment process in New South Wales, I also learned that many firm lawyers were eager to learn and obtain guidance on adoption of risk management systems. In particular, lawyers from smaller firms were interested in learning how to develop practice controls. But regardless of firm size, *Risk Management: Survival Tools for Law Firms* is an outstanding resource for lawyers seeking to develop an effective risk management system. The book not only poses important questions but gives lawyers user-friendly tools to help them evaluate and implement practice controls to improve the delivery of high-quality legal services while increasing firm profitability and lawyer satisfaction. This approach helps law firms not only to survive but to thrive.

Susan Fortney
Howard Lichtenstein Distinguished Professor of Legal Ethics
Director, Institute for the Study of Legal Ethics
Maurice Deane School of Law, Hofstra University

ACKNOWLEDGMENTS

We would like to thank everyone at the American Bar Association who assisted in the publication of this third edition, as well as our colleagues in the Lawyers for the Profession® practice at Hinshaw & Culbertson LLP for their continuing support.

ABOUT THE AUTHORS

Anthony E. Davis is a partner at Hinshaw & Culbertson, LLP, in New York City where he is the leader of the large law firm practice in the Lawyers for the Profession® practice group. He advises attorneys and law firms on legal professional and ethics issues, law firm creation, merger and dissolution, and issues relating to risk management and loss control. He is the co-author of *The Essential Formbook: Comprehensive Management Tools for Lawyers,* a four-volume series published by the ABA Law Practice Management Section.

Mr. Davis is a Lecturer-in-Law at Columbia University School of Law. Previously, as an adjunct professor of law, Mr. Davis taught Legal Profession at Brooklyn Law School for many years. He has also taught this course at the Benjamin N. Cardozo School of Law and at the University of Denver College of Law. In addition to his books, he has written and lectured widely on a variety of legal profession and ethics issues, including a regular bimonthly column on professional responsibility in the *New York Law Journal.* He is a past president of the Association of Professional Responsibility Lawyers, a fellow of the College of Law Practice Management, a fellow of the American Bar Foundation, and a member of the American Law Institute. Mr. Davis received his law degree from Cambridge University and his LLM from New York University School of Law. He is admitted in New York, Colorado, and as barrister (nonpracticing) and solicitor (nonpracticing) in England. He can be reached at adavis@hinshawlaw.com.

Katie M. Lachter is a partner in the New York office of Hinshaw & Culbertson, LLP, where she is a member of the Lawyers for the Profession® practice group. She defends attorneys in malpractice cases and disciplinary proceedings and advises lawyers, law firms, and in-house legal departments on issues relating to legal ethics and risk management.

Ms. Lachter is a Lecturer-in-Law at Columbia University School of Law, where she teaches Professional Responsibility. She is also on the faculty of the Practising Law Institute and Lawline.com. She is the co-author of a chapter entitled "The Practical Case for Civility," in *Essential Qualities of the Professional Lawyer,* published by the ABA Standing Committee on Professionalism in 2013. She has also co-authored numerous articles on ethics and professional responsibility for the *New York Law Journal* and Bloomberg law reports. Ms. Lachter is a past secretary of the New York City Bar Association Committee on Professional Ethics and a current member of the Association of Professional Responsibility Lawyers, the New York Women's Bar Association Ethics Committee, and the New York State Committee on Standards of Attorney Conduct (COSAC).

Ms. Lachter was named a 2012 Distinguished Legal Writing Award winner by the Burton Awards for Legal Achievement. She was also the recipient of the Legal Aid Society's 2009 Pro Bono Publico award. Ms. Lachter was designated a "Rising Star" by *Super Lawyers,* New York Metro Edition, in 2014 and named to the *Super Lawyers* list, New York Metro Edition, in 2015. She is admitted to practice in New York. She can be reached at klachter@hinshawlaw.com.

INTRODUCTION

The Legal Profession Today: Organized Bedlam or Orderly Evolution?

The legal profession in the second decade of the 21st century is facing unprecedented challenges from within—and, some would say, from without. It remains to be seen whether law firms in the United States can withstand the kinds of structural changes taking place in England and Australia (and showing strong signs of coming to Canada) that allow nonlawyers to act as firm owners, investors, and partners. But even apart from those game-changing structural and organizational shifts, American lawyers are facing many pressures: to satisfy clients who demand value billing, to expand (and streamline) their firms, to specialize, to change the way members of the profession are educated and trained, to change how they are compensated, and on and on.[1]

While some would deny that the hourly fee model of billing (and the balance of power between seller and buyer of legal services that this model represents) needs to be rethought, the drop in realization defined by billing rates and by collections and the reduction in average hours billed by partners by hundreds of hours per year over the same period show that something has to give in the way firms operate if they are to prosper. The rush to merge, to move laterally, to change from general service to boutique, to differentiate by fee structure, to move the back offices, and to outsource all indicate that the old ways are changing, and if law firms are to survive, they will have to adapt. Meanwhile, all this change is happening in a workplace being transformed by advances in technology: work that might have been performed by a team of associates ten years ago can now be done by one lawyer and a group of software experts (predictive coding in document review); there are software programs that can compare multiple sophisticated contracts in a few minutes; clients can access the same research tools as their lawyers with equal ease and speed. The ramifications of the effects of technology are only dimly beginning to be understood by those trying to figure out what the law firm of the future will do, how it will do it—and who will be the people providing the service. If we can see that firms organized in a pyramid, and relying on leverage, are dinosaurs, we cannot clearly see what will be the successful models that will replace them.

And even as the structure of how legal services will be provided is changing before our eyes, the practice of law is becoming increasingly risky. Suits against lawyers by clients and nonclients are commonplace, as multimillion-dollar settlements and verdicts continue at a steady pace. So do criminal and disciplinary proceedings. And no one—not solo practitioners, not small firms with a single office, and not mega-firms with many offices—can claim immunity. But those are just the traditional threats. A thoughtlessly worded e-mail can go viral on the Internet and cause untold reputational and financial harm to a law firm. With the application of the Health Insurance Portability and Account-ability Act to law firms, regulators unheard of just a few years ago have come onto the scene; they can direct how firms operate (and thereby add significantly to the cost of doing business), impose sanctions, and potentially cause the firm to actually lose business. As a result, as we will discuss in chapter 1, the very meaning of risk in a law practice is geometrically broader than it was even when the second edition of this work was published in 2007. Indeed, there is a new catchphrase that neatly sums up the different nature, scope, and severity of the risks fac-ing law firms: *enterprise risk management*. Managing risk is no longer just about avoiding malpractice claims or professional discipline. Rather, it is about understanding the new universe of threats that can undermine a law firm's reputation and ability to exist.

Lawyers cannot afford to turn their back on these developments or act as if the risks do not exist. Even if it was once true that clients would always stand by their lawyers, and that every lawyer's word was his or her bond, that is not the world of today. Furthermore, it would be a dis-service to clients, to lawyers, and to the legal system to ignore the posi-tive opportunities presented by recent changes. For example, access to computerized legal research that makes it easier for lawyers all over the country to provide highly competent legal services should be viewed as a plus. The question before us is not whether to accept the present or when the past will return. The question before us is how best to keep abreast of developments so that we can serve the interests of our clients, our legal system, and—yes—ourselves.

LAW FIRM ORGANIZATION: FROM PARTNERSHIP TO CORPORATION

The idealized model for law firms in previous eras was the "true" part-nership, in which lawyers at a firm knew one another and got along with one another. They also had the time and energy to know what the other partners were doing. In this idyllic and much slower-paced world, the partners could make decisions as a group and with much less con-cern about competitive pressures or risks of liability.

By contrast, most contemporary law firms delegate at least some authority among ostensible equals and make significant use of nonlaw-yer administrators. Some degree of centralized management and con-trol is thus a fact of life for almost all lawyers and perhaps the most predominant fact of life for lawyers in larger firms. Some firms are espousing what is coming to be referred to unashamedly as corporate governance.

Most of us lack the time, interest, or ability to return to the true partnership era of the past, but we still have important choices to make. Law firms, like other businesses, can be run poorly or well. Lawyers at a firm can have good systems to help manage risk and can make good use of those systems, or they can have systems that exist in name only. Potentially serious errors can be analyzed to provide lessons for the future, or they can be ignored.

Proper risk management for law firms thus consists of adopting and implementing controls that are appropriate to the risks faced by a lawyer or firm and of developing a law firm culture that is conscious of these risks and the need to avoid them. "Zero risk" is generally unattainable. For lawyers in most settings, however, an acceptable level of risk should be within reach.

But recognizing the risks that confront us is only half the battle. The real challenge is to understand what is meant by *management*. Perhaps the clearest example of the significance of that challenge is to be found in the sad story of the demise of the once venerable firm of Jenkins and Gilchrist. The essence of the story is that the firm, seeking to expand beyond its Texas roots, merged with a boutique in Chicago that specialized in tax shelter work. The new practice was incredibly profitable, such that the small additional team of lawyers dramatically improved the entire firm's profitability—and its standing in the league tables otherwise known as the AmLaw rankings. The tax shelters drew scrutiny from the Internal Revenue Service. The firm accurately identified the risks of the work being performed and regularly discussed whether those risks were acceptable. But the money proved too enticing, and instead of putting a stop to the risky practices, the firm looked the other way. The government intervened and effectively forced the entire firm to close.[2] This story provides a perfect example of a firm whose managers recognized an enterprise-threatening risk yet utterly failed to manage.[3]

While the story of Jenkins and Gilchrist is seminal, many might respond by saying, "Well, that could never happen at our law firm." The problem is that law firm managers are challenged every day by the need to manage the most basic risk that law firms face: selecting good clients and avoiding bad ones. It should be (and often is) obvious whether and when a firm should refuse business, but imposing management insight and will on lawyers who perceive themselves as being rewarded based on their book of business is often impossible. This challenge—which is not new—is becoming increasingly amenable to improved management techniques and software. But if a firm's management is not empowered to *manage*, all the sophistication and software in the world will not save the firm.

Consider, for example, a lawyer who agrees to represent someone who turns out to be dishonest or otherwise unworthy and who subsequently sues the firm, causes the firm to be sued by third parties, or simply takes off with substantial unpaid receivables.[4] It is easy, after the fact, to blame the lawyer for not conducting greater due diligence before taking this person on as a client, for not managing the client-lawyer relationship more effectively, or for not reacting to red flags that were or should have been visible along the way. It is rarely the case, however, that the lawyer is the only one who deserves the blame. And what's more, a firm that does not consider how its overall culture and systems may directly or indirectly have contributed to the problem, and that does not take steps to prevent a recurrence, will unquestionably run a higher risk that this painful history will repeat itself. To avoid such a problem, a firm might well wish to ask itself the following questions:

- *Is our system for client intake and new business review adequate?* Before accepting a client, can and should we take additional steps to make it easier to detect and reject high-risk clients? Do we have the right people performing the client intake function, and are they adequately compensated for saying no as well as yes? And if we have the right people, does the firm allow them to be bullied by key partners or practice groups? If the particular problem in this case should have been caught but somehow slipped through the cracks, how do we avoid similar problems in the future? Have we ever mined our past data to see how we might improve our future performance?
- *Does our compensation system encourage or permit individual lawyers to take risks that are inappropriate from the firm's point of view?* Does our compensation system, including but not limited to our hourly quotas or guidelines, lead lawyers who do not have enough work on their plates to take on work that they are not qualified to do or that should properly be handled by other lawyers at the firm? Alternatively, does our system lead lawyers to overwork matters in a way that either turns off clients or results in client refusals to pay?
- *What is the firm's general approach to "cowboy" or other errant lawyers?* Are they treated as heroes—or deferred to as the firm's eight-hundred-pound gorillas? Do they occupy key managerial positions? Are they encouraged or allowed to ignore firm practices or policies that others must obey? Does anyone at the firm have responsibility to make sure there is an appropriate matching between the work to be done and the skills of the lawyers selected to do it?
- *Were there points along the way when we collectively did see or could have seen what was coming and avoided adverse consequence?* What, if anything, does the firm do when an account falls 60 or 90 days past due? To what extent, if any, does the firm monitor high-profile or other cases on an ongoing basis? Are lawyers encouraged to discuss difficult problems with others, or is seeking assistance viewed as a sign of weakness?
- *When people are aware of a brewing problem, are they encouraged to step forward?* What would happen to a staff member, associate, or junior partner who expressed doubts to a senior partner about the conduct of another senior partner? And, just as important, what do our staff members, associates, or junior partners *think* would happen?

Or consider a firm that finds itself on the wrong end of a conflicts claim. If blame is simply heaped on the unfortunate—and perhaps ill-advised—lawyer who took in the matter giving rise to the conflict, much important information may be lost. For example, the firm might wish to ask a number of questions:

- *Do we have a user-friendly conflicts-checking system?* Is it easy or hard for lawyers to get conflicts data into the system and to understand the results that the system gives back? Are the responses produced in a timely way? Is help readily available for lawyers who may or do need it?

- *Does our system contain the necessary data?* Do lawyers provide the names of clients (or adversaries) and pertinent related parties?
- *How difficult (or easy) is it for a lawyer to make an end run around the system?* Can work on a file be started, or even completed, before conflicts checks are run? Before oral or written waivers are obtained? If the answer to any of these questions is yes, what steps should the firm take to see to it that someone follows up on these matters? Is recourse available within the firm when a lawyer delays or refuses to contact his or her client to seek a waiver for the benefit of another lawyer and client?
- *Does the firm have workable and intelligible policies for when it will or will not proceed with or without conflicts waivers?* Has the firm drawn, and recently reviewed, policies or practices to separate overly risky situations from less risky ones? Are these policies or practices actually known to firm attorneys? What steps does the firm take to update the policies or practices as needed? How does the firm inform attorneys about recent case law developments? How does the firm ensure that new or laterally hired attorneys fully understand how things are done?
- *How well do we document conflicts waivers?* Does the firm make form letters available to lawyers who wish to use them? Do the letters just say "this will confirm that you have consented," or do they address the substantive issues underlying the need for waivers? Is any time spent in reviewing the letters to see whether the firm's lawyers actually practice what the firm's policies preach?

Anyone can be deceived or make a mistake. And anyone can be the victim of unforeseen forces that are beyond meaningful control. Fortunately, however, most risks that lawyers face are neither unforeseeable nor uncontrollable. The most important question that a firm's lawyers and nonlawyers should ask one another and their firm is this: where do we wish to stand on issues of ethics and risk management, and how do we make sure that we are the firm we want to be?

THE RISE OF LAW FIRM GENERAL COUNSEL

A critically important change in addressing both aspects of the challenge (identifying and managing risk) has been law firms' almost universal recognition of the need for a professional in-firm counsel. The significance of that position is discussed in chapter 1. But the advent of the firm's general counsel may well prove to be but a staging post along the way. For law firms that recognize the implications of enterprise risk, the next step—following the model of their corporate clients—is likely to be the *Office* of General Counsel. If the risks are increasing exponentially, then the job will be (and in many firms already is) too large for an individual to handle. For instance, if a firm has offices around the world, what happens when a problem erupts in a jurisdiction where the middle of the day there is the middle of the night for the general counsel?

Creating a skilled staff ready, willing, and able to address the panoply of risks on a 24/7 basis 365 days a year will become essential. In turn, the cost of managing risk will necessarily grow—which, of course, brings us back to the beginning of this introduction. Firms able and willing to bear the burden of those sunk costs must be ready and able to be profitable in the changing marketplace for legal services.

LEGAL AND PERSONAL ACCOUNTABILITY

In all this talk of management, however, we should not lose sight of the fundamental principles that will continue to underlie the operation of law firms as long as their personnel aspire to be deemed professionals: individual responsibility and accountability. However much a firm seeks to understand and manage risk, it will ultimately succeed only when all employees are accountable for their own conduct and act as their brothers' and sisters' keeper.

LO AND BEHOLD, RISK MANAGEMENT WORKS

In chapter 2, we present a case study from New South Wales, Australia, demonstrating that the risk management practices we have promoted for years actually work. While we have previously presented anecdotal data showing the effectiveness of risk management, we now have a longitudinal study *proving that risk management reduces claims against law firms.* There is no better time for law firms in the United States to start making use of these techniques or to continue to improve their risk management practices. Chapter 3 sets forth the main elements of risk management for lawyers and law firms, while chapters 4 and 5 discuss the role of law firm audits and how law firms can successfully implement a risk management process.

Part 2 of this book consists of nine questionnaires designed to aid firms in undertaking a self-audit. These materials are referred to collectively as QUIC (Quality/In Control) Surveys, and they are designed to offer a specific solution to firms interested in improving their risk management. Part 3 contains a corresponding answer and analysis (crib) sheet for each of the questionnaires in part 2.

NOTES

1. Georgetown Law Center for the Study of the Legal Profession & Peer Monitor, 2013 Report on the State of the Legal Market (Thomson Reuters 2013).

2. Nathan Koppel, *How a Bid to Boost Profits Led to a Law Firm's Demise*, Wall St. J., May 17, 2007, at A1.

3. *See* Tanina Rostain & Milton C. Regan Jr., Confidence Games (MIT Press 2014).

4. This section is drawn from Peter R. Jarvis, *Learning from Rocket Science*, Professional Lawyer, summer 2004, at 26.

PART 1

Law Firm Management in a Hostile Environment: A Guide to Risk Management

CHAPTER 1

What Is Risk Management (or Loss Prevention) Anyway?

RISK

There are two ways to look at risk management.

The definition of "risk" used in previous editions of this book was "any danger that, if not controlled, may lead to consequences unintended by and harmful to a law firm or practitioner. This includes professional discipline, malpractice or other claims for disgorgement of fees or money damages, and other allegations of wrongful conduct in the course of law practice."

But there is another view that is frequently easier to "sell" to lawyers and law firms. If the object of a law firm is to provide legal services to clients and generate fees with which to reward the firm's lawyers, then risk is "*anything* that interferes with the ability of the firm and its lawyers to provide legal services and generate profit from doing so."

One way of making the subject of risk concrete is to relate it to the subject of fee disputes. Let us count the ways in which a simple fee dispute involves risk.

- Every moment a lawyer has to spend fighting to collect a fee that she believes she has already earned could be spent doing productive and billable work for another client.
- If a lawyer or firm is in the middle of a fee dispute while a matter is ongoing, a huge barrier has been raised that impedes the ability of the lawyer to provide—or the client to accept—ongoing legal services. Fee disputes erode the trust that is the essential glue of a productive attorney-client relationship.
- If the dispute rises to the point where the firm sues the client for its fee (or the client, anticipating such a move, initiates a malpractice claim), all kinds of additional risks arise. First, even if the virtually inevitable malpractice claim is meritless, the firm must notify and probably make a claim under its professional liability policy (even though the policy will not cover the fees or costs associated with the fee claim, or the loss of fees). Second, there is usually a reason that clients refuse to pay: either they lack the funds or they

have a legitimate complaint. Either way, the firm may well not recover any of the missing fee. Meanwhile, the cost of pursuing such claims in human terms (the loss of more time that could have been billed to paying clients) and in hiring a lawyer or losing the productive value of a litigator from within the firm will diminish the value of even a completely successful outcome or, more likely, will equal or outweigh the ultimate value of even a partially successful outcome.

But the risks of fee disputes do not end there.

- Once a lawsuit starts, the parties are entitled to *discovery*. Now the client looks at every scrap of information in the firm's files, including the time sheets and e-mails among lawyers. If there's an ill-considered entry or e-mail, the client shifts from claiming malpractice to alleging fraudulent billing. That allegation very quickly hits the media.[1] So now the firm faces two additional risks: damage to its reputation and the questioning of its billing practices by *every* client.

This example demonstrates that risk is pervasive in the operation of every law firm, but, if properly managed, the firm can serve clients well and be profitable. In risk management terms, and as discussed in the Introduction, this means first that the firm must do more effective client intake management to identify clients who are likely to prove problematic and to limit intake to clients that the firm is best equipped to serve and who are able and most likely willing to pay for those services. Second, the firm should use clear and comprehensive engagement letters to describe the scope of services to be provided. Third, the firm should manage the billing and collection process actively to identify problem clients before the amount at issue is great and to consider withdrawing from representation and abandoning the fee claim as the quickest way of avoiding a problem and getting back to productive work. Finally, if the decision, for whatever reason, is to proceed with a suit, the firm should take the time to review all the work performed to assess the merits of the inevitable malpractice counterclaim as well as time and billing records and internal communications to make sure that the potential for embarrassment does not outweigh even a large account receivable.

If we were to discuss the traditional risk of malpractice claims, many of the same considerations would apply, including the financial costs implicated in defending claims, hidden costs such as time and billings lost from productive activities, damage to reputation, and increased future costs of insurance. Accordingly, recognizing that every client and matter carries potential costs as well as profit gives substance to the meaning of risk in law practice. The actual management and oversight of the way services are delivered, and of the lawyers who are providing those services, are an equally important component of a risk management program. Here again, managing the delivery of legal services enables law firms to make *positive* virtue out of risk management—serving clients better and generating more profit.

RISK MANAGEMENT

The term "risk management" refers to the establishment of institutional (firm- or practice-wide) policies, procedures, or systems (sometimes called risk management tools) designed to identify and minimize risk within the firm and its practice.

Ideally, every risk management tool (policy, procedure, or system) should

- establish uniform standards
- be capable of ready monitoring for compliance
- involve the minimum of intrusion and expense into other operations of the law practice consistent with maintaining the efficacy of the tool

To be effective, risk management in law firms requires more than the development and application of risk management tools. The firm must also have a culture that both promotes awareness of the kinds of risks that the firm's practice necessarily entails and actively supports compliance with the policies and procedures that the firm has adopted. Of course, it is impossible to eliminate or avoid all risk. Law firms can, however, realistically seek to manage risk within acceptable parameters.

LOSS PREVENTION

"Loss prevention" and "loss control" are more traditional terms used by the professional liability insurance industry, and they are synonymous with risk management. It is worth noting in this context that risk management is not a new phenomenon to anyone—except, relatively speaking, to lawyers. If you reflect on the history of the insurance industry, going back even to its roots in Lloyd's coffee parlor in London in the 18th century, a crucial element of underwriting has always been to seek to reduce the insurance risk by improving the safety of the product or service being insured. Because the shipping industry was the first to seek insurance, there was a drive to improve shipbuilding and navigation techniques. Subsequently, improving safety has become a key element of all underwriting; hard hats for construction workers and seat belts and air bags for passengers in automobiles are obvious examples of modern-day risk management tools generated, or at least strongly supported, by insurers.

Risk management is so well developed in the accounting profession that it goes beyond the elements suggested in this book, often involving regularly scheduled mandatory external reviews—conducted by competitor firms. This comparison is important because it helps to correct the mistaken notion that risk management is needed, and effective, only when a product (such as an architect's plans) or a risk to life and health (such as a doctor's treatment) is involved.

WHY RISK MANAGEMENT MATTERS

Addressing this foundational question, one of the authors wrote in an article about this subject (referred to hereafter as the "Davis Georgetown article"):[2]

> There are four reasons why law firms take risk management seriously. First, it enables them to improve the quality of the services they provide to their clients; second, and following from the delivery of improved services, it enables them to achieve greater profitability; third, the adoption of effective risk management systems gives law firms enhanced access to the professional liability insurance market; and, fourth, risk management, as the words suggest, helps law firms to identify and manage risks which, if not addressed, present the threat of significant adverse consequences.

It is vital to recognize that the first two objectives are in every sense positive incentives. Almost by definition, lawyers are generally hostile to being managed and to accepting management responsibility. The usual refrains from lawyers are, "No one is going to tell me how to practice law" and "I didn't go to law school in order to become a manager." To get law firms and lawyers to accept the principles of risk management, it is important to demonstrate that it is in their individual and collective self-interest to do so. Accordingly, all risk management systems, policies, and procedures need to be designed and implemented in ways that actively assist lawyers in providing professional services and that, to the greatest extent possible, demonstrably improve efficiency and profitability. Not unrelated to the issue of profitability is the third reason law firms take risk management seriously—their professional liability insurers either require them to do so or take positive note when they do so of their own volition. From its origins in a coffee shop in London, insurance has always had as its key component the management of risk. Professional liability insurers have learned that the practice of law is in this respect no different from a construction site. Just as insurers require construction workers to wear hard hats, they are increasingly focused on law firms' adoption of appropriate risk management systems, from client intake through practice management. The availability of coverage, the size of deductibles, the limits available, the terms of coverage, and the price of malpractice insurance are more and more dependent on law firms' ability to demonstrate to underwriters that they have adopted and institutionalized appropriate risk management systems.

The next two sections of this chapter are also taken in part from the Davis Georgetown article.

LAW FIRM GENERAL COUNSEL: THE CRITICAL PREREQUISITE FOR EFFECTIVE RISK MANAGEMENT

The most important component of an effective risk management structure in law firms is the designation of a general counsel. The role traditionally had a variety of labels, including ethics partner, risk management, or loss prevention partner. The importance of this role derives from its four essential functions. The first and most important function of the individual designated as general counsel is to act as the law firm's "lightning rod." In other words, the general counsel's first responsibility is to be entirely open to receiving reports of any kind of problematic issue that might constitute a risk to the firm in the broadest sense, as defined above. The sooner problems are identified, the more likely they are to be resolved without serious adverse consequences. Accordingly, the person selected to act as general counsel must have strong interpersonal skills, as well as the appropriate background or training in legal ethics and professional responsibility. The second function is to act as the firm's lawyer, and in particular to advise management on all issues relating to professional responsibility. A vital subset of this second function is the oversight of client intake—and particularly the resolution of all conflicts of interest. The third function is to oversee the defense of claims asserted against the firm and its lawyers. The fourth function is to develop, promulgate, and enforce appropriate risk management policies, procedures, and systems throughout the law firm.

Just as important as the designation of a general counsel are the development of a policy and the training of all lawyers and staff relating to their individual obligations toward the general counsel. It is vital that employees understand that their loyalty obligations are not to individual superiors but (1) to the firm's clients, to protect them from any form of inadequate service or inappropriate conduct; (2) to individuals in the firm, whether to render needed assistance or to prevent them from pursuing inappropriate goals; and (3) to the firm itself, to protect its reputation. Because these priorities may not always be obvious to any given individual lawyer or staff member, an explicit policy dealing with reporting obligations, as well as training of new hires at every level of the firm and regular reinforcement of these values, is essential to the establishment of an effective risk management culture within a law firm.

HOW RISK MANAGEMENT HELPS FIRMS SERVE CLIENTS BETTER, IMPROVE PROFITABILITY, OPTIMIZE ACCESS TO INSURANCE, AND IDENTIFY AND MANAGE RISKS

A prime example illustrating how risk management systems can help to accomplish all four of these objectives when effectively implemented—and avoid the kinds of risks that all too frequently arise in the absence of such systems and of an appropriately supportive culture—is client intake management. As explained in the Davis Georgetown article,

> [w]hen lawyers accept engagements from clients who subsequently sue their firms, leave their firms with substantial unpaid receivables, or cause their firms to be sued by disgruntled third parties, it is all too easy to blame the individual lawyers for poor client selection and lack of adequate due diligence. In reality, however, when these situations arise it is usually the absence of

effective and appropriately supported risk management systems within the firm at large that is the real culprit. Furthermore, firms that fail to consider either the adequacy of their client intake management infrastructure or the adequacy of the firm's culture in supporting and encouraging compliance by its lawyers with its chosen systems unquestionably increase the likelihood that such painful episodes will endlessly recur.

If a law firm wishes to have a client intake management system that enables it both to represent clients it can profitably and effectively serve and to avoid engagements with inappropriate clients, then the firm will have to address four broad issues:

1. Does the Firm Require Every Lawyer Seeking to Accept an Engagement from a New Client to Obtain Adequate Information about the Prospective Client?

Law firms that have sought to perfect their client intake systems have found that they must obtain four distinct kinds of information about prospective engagements. First, is the new engagement likely to involve the firm in any kind of conflict of interest, broadly defined? Second, is the engagement one within the competence and expertise of both the firm and the individual lawyers who will work on the matter? Third, does the client have the means to pay fees appropriate to the successful conclusion of the matter? Fourth, are there any indications that the client will prove to be otherwise unworthy or inappropriate or will present special risks to the law firm?

If a firm desires an effective intake review, then the firm's management or its designees, independent of the introducing partner, should assess all new clients regarding each of these issues, based on adequate information that the introducing lawyer must produce as a prerequisite for the firm's evaluation. Such information might cover the following subjects:

Identity of the Client. Analysis of malpractice claims reveals two common causes of disputes between lawyers and clients. First, when representing entities, especially small or closely held businesses, the lawyer believes that she represents the entity but the individual owners or principals believe that the firm is representing them individually and owes them independent duties of care. And since the determining factor will be what the plaintiff reasonable believes, the law firm will usually be on the short end of the stick. Similarly, when lawyers take on multiple clients in the same matter (joint representation), absent extremely carefully worded and comprehensive disclosure and waiver language, the resulting conflicts of interest can be fatal to any defense. For these reasons, the use of engagement letters that address this issue is critical.

Competence. It sounds trite, but it isn't. Lawyers' professional liability insurers refer to the problem of taking on inappropriate work as "dabbling." Especially in hard economic times, law firms and individual lawyers do it to show that they are busy or at least occupied. But taking on work that is outside a firm's or an individual lawyer's area of competence invites trouble. At best, even if a successful outcome is achieved, it will often be impossible to generate a fee that does not enrage the client because of the cost of the learning curve necessary to get there. But even more problematic is the greatly increased risk that malpractice will be committed precisely because of the unfamiliarity of the subject matter.

Scope of Services. It is critical that both the lawyer and the client understand precisely what services the lawyer will provide—and the limits of those services. Absent this clarity, and wherever there is uncertainty, the problem of the client's reasonable belief crops up again.[3]

This concept of limiting the scope of employment is hardly revolutionary. Rule 1.2 of the Model Rules implicitly recognizes the parties' right to control the scope of representation, and the commentary to Rule 1.2(a) states this explicitly:

> The scope of services to be provided by a lawyer may be limited by agreement with the client or by the terms under which the lawyer's services are made available to the client. . . . In addition, the terms upon which representation is undertaken may exclude specific means that might otherwise be used to accomplish the client's objectives. *Such limitations may exclude actions . . . that the lawyer regards as repugnant or imprudent.* [Emphasis added.]

Assignment of Staff. Given discussions of competence and scope of services, it follows that, whatever the urgings of the introducing partner (whose practice may be in an entirely different field) or even of the client, the firm needs to retain the authority to assign lawyers competent to work on the matter. Clearly, such a requirement is part of the same duty to provide competent counsel.

Ability to Pay. Every client comes with a potential price tag of at least the amount of the firm's insurance deductible, so the question whether the client can pay the bills is of heightened significance. Left to their individual devices, and without independent review of this aspect of intake, individual lawyers will all too often ignore it and take on impecunious clients just to stay "busy."

Engagement Letters. The fact that some lawyers and firms continue to resist the use of written engagement letters does nothing to reduce the importance of such letters or their value to those who use them.

The need for a written engagement letter is emphasized by a New York case involving the leading bankruptcy firm of Weil, Gotshal & Manges. The firm had accepted an engagement subject to an oral limitation that it would not be required to represent this particular client in any issue relating to lender liability because doing so might require the firm to take positions adverse to the interests of the firm's other clients.

Because the limitation was not in writing, the court explicitly declined to allow the firm to withdraw from the engagement when the client sought to have the firm assert lender liability claims.[4]

2. Has the Firm Developed an Appropriate Managerial Screening System That Enables It to Undertake Independent Review of Every Prospective Engagement?

There are three vital attributes of a successful client intake management screen. First, with respect to every new client and each new matter for new and existing clients, there must be an independent review on the part of the firm of the information provided by the lawyer seeking to open the matter. Firms establish such mechanisms in a variety of ways: by committees, by delegating the function to practice leaders, and, most efficiently, by establishing an independent new client and matter intake review structure. Second, this independent review must assess all four of the information groups discussed in item 1 (conflicts, competence, ability to pay fees, and client worthiness). Third, this management process must operate in real time with sufficient speed to enable the firm to make the necessary judgments before work is commenced on the prospective new matter.

In addition, when potential issues are raised as to the advisability of acceptance of a particular matter or client, the system must provide for the speediest possible review and resolution of such issues. For instance, if conflict waivers are required, not only should standard forms be available, but help in drafting appropriate disclosure and waiver language should also be readily available from the general counsel's office.

3. Does the Firm's Culture Appropriately Reward Compliance with Its Client Intake System—and Punish Noncompliance?

There are many ways in which law firm culture can operate to enhance or, in the worst instances, effectively disable client intake management systems. For example, compensation structures, such as those that operate on an "eat what you kill" basis, are likely to lead lawyers to try to undermine or avoid independent review of the decision to bring on new work. Similarly, hourly quotas or guidelines may encourage lawyers with insufficient work at any given moment to seek to take on matters that they are unqualified to handle. A culture that treats the firm's most powerful partners as heroes and encourages or permits them to ignore established client intake management oversight systems serves to undermine those systems, often rendering them useless in the situations when they are most needed. In contrast, compensation structures that reward collegial behavior and adherence to firm policies and systems are likely to gain the most utility from those systems. One among many indications that a firm's culture appropriately encourages adherence to client intake management procedures is a well-established general counsel whose role in overseeing client intake generally, and the resolution of conflicts of interest specifically, is well understood throughout the firm.

4. Does the Client Intake System Encourage a Positive Relationship between the Client and the Lawyers Who Will Be Providing Service?

There are two discrete elements of a client intake system that can be made "user friendly" from the client's perspective. First, the initial client intake interview or meeting must be thorough to fully develop the information required for the firm to make its intake decision, as discussed in item 1. This is important from the client's perspective because it demonstrates that the firm is serious, interested in examining the prospective client's problem, and in making a considered decision as to whether it can assist the prospective client, as opposed to a cursory discussion giving rise to the belief on the part of the prospective client that the law firm is principally interested in the matter as a source of fees. Similarly, effective client intake management should require the preparation of an engagement letter, following an approved form that details all the essential aspects of the prospective engagement. Well-crafted letters help to establish realistic expectations on the part of the client. The system should also require the client's countersignature as a condition for undertaking the engagement.

ADDITIONAL RISK MANAGEMENT TOOLS

Practice Group Management

One risk management structure that large firms have increasingly adopted in recent years is the establishment, or development of the role, of practice groups. In some firms practice groups continue to be seen mostly as a collective marketing vehicle. In fact, they can—and should—be used to oversee the nature and quality of the services being provided to clients. For many reasons, practice group management—properly implemented—should be considered a positive and integral part of the way a firm practices law and provides services to its clients. First, it is the only way to be assured of maintaining a universally high standard of client service over time. Second, it forms the basis for continuous training of all lawyers within the group. Third, it enables firms to incorporate clients into the risk management structure rather than leaving them, like separate and untouchable fiefdoms, within the personal domain of individual partners. Fourth, in a well-organized practice group, when mistakes are made, they can be identified and dealt with promptly—and almost always before devolving into calamities and crises. Fifth, effective practice management is a tool for improving profitability, both because it focuses marketing efforts and because it makes for satisfied clients, who in turn pay their bills, bring additional business, and refer other clients. Accordingly, when presented to the outside world as part of a firm's commitment to providing work of consistently high quality, this aspect of risk management has the potential for becoming a positive marketing tool.

Firm Management and Risk Management Oversight

An absolutely critical—but too often overlooked—element in the risk management equation is the need for law firm management to actively manage the firms' lawyers. All too many firms can attest to the perils of failing to manage and oversee all of their partners, especially their senior "heavy hitting" ones. Indeed, in the last several years a few prominent firms have faced the public dissemination of allegations of a senior partner's engaging in improper or outright fraudulent billing practices. If such activities in fact occurred, it would suggest that the firms' management structures were incapable of identifying or controlling these practices. Many of the other large claims against law firms attest to the continuing shortcomings in the way that firms actually manage what their lawyers do and how they behave.

For risk management practices to succeed, it is essential that the need for risk management be accepted by everyone in a firm, from the most powerful partner on down. A program that is recognized as being for the common good can operate as an effective brake on dangerous activities, including engagements having the potential to harm the firm.

As discussed earlier in this chapter, many firms (including almost all large firms) have institutionalized their risk management functions by appointing a general counsel for the firm. There can no longer be any doubt that a properly empowered, appropriately staffed, adequately supplied office of general counsel is a critical component of risk management for those firms. Apart from functioning as a lightning rod for the early identification and resolution of problems and issues, the general counsel should also monitor all other components of the firm's risk management policies, procedures, and systems, from client intake to file destruction.

NOTES

1. Nathan Koppel, *A Lawyer's Charges Open Window on Bill Padding by Law Firms*, Wall St. J., Aug. 30, 2006.
2. Anthony E. Davis, *Legal Ethics and Risk Management: Complementary Visions of Lawyer Regulation*, 21 Geo. J. Legal Ethics 95 (2008).
3. *See* AmBase Corp. v. Davis Polk & Wardwell, 8 N.Y.3d 428, 866 N.E.2d 1033 (2007).
4. Heller Fin., Inc. v. Apple Tree Realty Assocs., 1994 WL 16858121 (N.Y. Sup. Ct. Nov. 18, 1994) (order).

CHAPTER 2

A Working Model of Pervasive Risk Management: New South Wales, Australia

Remarkably—to American lawyers—the utility of risk management generally, and of self-audits specifically, has already been empirically established *and proven.*

In 2004, New South Wales in Australia enacted the Legal Profession Act 2004, governing incorporated legal practices and multidisciplinary partnerships. Under section 140 of the Act, law firms that opt to incorporate are required "to ensure that appropriate management systems are implemented and maintained." To enable law firms to demonstrate compliance with the Act, the regulator of the legal profession, the Office of the Legal Services Commissioner (OLSC), in conjunction with the Council of the Law Society (LSC) and others, created a self-assessment form for firms to use. The OLSC's form covers ten areas in which firms must rate themselves to determine whether they have "appropriate management systems" in place.

These areas, described below, closely track the risk management categories described in chapter 1 (with the exception of undertakings):

1. Competent work practices to avoid negligence
2. Effective, timely, and courteous communication
3. Timely delivery, review, and follow-up of legal services to avoid delay
4. Acceptable processes for liens and file transfers
5. Shared understanding and appropriate documentation from commencement through termination of retainer regarding cost closure, billing practices, and termination of retainer
6. Timely identification of conflicts of interest, which may arise when acting for both parties or acting against previous clients, and potential conflicts of interest, which may arise in relationships with debt collectors and mercantile agencies or when conducting another business, collecting referral fees and commissions, and so on
7. Records management
8. Undertakings (binding commitments made by lawyers on behalf of their clients)
9. Supervision of practice and staff
10. Trust accounts

Every firm regulated by the OLSC must assess its compliance by completing the form, a copy of which appears at the end of this chapter. Notably, the form is short—just ten pages of "objectives"; for each one, firms must assess whether they are not compliant, partially compliant, compliant, fully compliant, or fully compliant plus. For every rating of not compliant or partially compliant, the firms must explain what actions they will take to achieve compliance.

A study conducted in 2008 to measure the impact of the self-assessment requirement showed that the rate of complaints for firms (and their lawyers) subject to this regime went down by two-thirds after their initial self-assessment using the regulator's form.[1] Notable also was the finding, in the same study, that the rate of complaints for the regulated entities was *one-third* the rate for those in nonregulated practices.[2] A follow-up study likewise found "a significant reduction of the number of complaints filed against lawyers" in the regulated firms.[3] Although beyond the scope of this book, these studies and related articles, most notably the seminal essay by Professor Ted Schneyer, *Professional Discipline in Law Firms*,[4] strongly suggest that management-based principles "can help transform a lawyer disciplinary system from a reactive one to a proactive one that educates and assists lawyers in conducting their practices ethically and efficiently."[5] The authors recommend reading these articles and those cited therein to better appreciate the enormous value to be gained by undertaking self-assessments (or audits), both to encourage ethical behavior by individual lawyers and to improve the efficiency and effectiveness of law firm management systems.

The self-assessment form is a principle-based approach intended to apply generally to all regulated firms. The tables that follow show the questions that firms must ask themselves to determine their compliance level in each of the relevant categories.

SELF-ASSESSMENT OF "APPROPRIATE MANAGEMENT SYSTEMS" FOR INCORPORATED LEGAL PRACTICES IN NEW SOUTH WALES

Section 140(3)(a) of the *Legal Profession Act 2004* (the Act) requires legal practitioner directors of incorporated legal practices (ILPs) to ensure that "appropriate management systems" are implemented and maintained to ensure that the provision of legal services by ILPs complies with the requirements of the Act, the *Legal Profession Regulation 2005* (the Regulations) and the *New South Wales Professional Conduct and Practice Rules 2013* (the Solicitors' Rules). Failure to comply can amount to professional misconduct. The OLSC and the LSC of New South Wales (NSW) each has power under the Act (Chapter 6) to investigate or audit ILPs in connection with the provision of legal services.

Although the Act does not define "appropriate management systems," the OLSC, working collaboratively with LSC, LawCover, and the College of Law, has adopted an "education towards compliance" strategy to assist ILPs to fulfil their professional obligations. This self-assessment form addresses ten areas that the OLSC suggests should be addressed in considering "appropriate management systems." The ten areas are referred to as "objectives" in the first, left-hand column of the form.

The self-assessment form requires legal practitioner directors to assess the systems in place in their practices by rating them by comparison with the examples that are given in the third column of the form. **All examples provided in this document are suggestions only.** The OLSC recognizes that ILPs vary in terms of size and work practices. Legal practitioner directors are encouraged to contact the OLSC or the LSC of NSW for any clarification needed or additional examples.

Please consider *each key concept* and rate your practice as either "not compliant," "partially compliant," "compliant," "fully compliant," or "fully compliant plus" ("NC/PC/C/FC/FC PLUS" respectively). If you rate your practice NC or PC please outline the action you will take to achieve compliance. If you use an alternate system or procedure from the examples described in this form, please describe it. **If you believe any of the key concepts are not applicable, please note them as being not applicable (N/A) and provide reasons why that is the case.**

Self-Assessment Ratings Explained

Self-Assessment Rating	Code	Explanation
Not Compliant	NC	Not all objectives have been addressed.
Partially Compliant	PC	All objectives have been addressed but the management systems for achieving these objectives are not fully functional.
Compliant	C	Management systems exist for all objectives and are fully functional.
Fully Compliant	FC	Management systems exist for all objectives and all are fully functional and all are regularly assessed for effectiveness.
Fully Compliant Plus	FC Plus	All objectives have been addressed, all management systems are documented and all are fully functional and all are assessed regularly for effectiveness, plus improvements are made when needed.
Not Compliant	(N/A)	Objective or key concept within an objective does not apply to the ILP. Provide a reason why you have given this rating.

Self-Assessment Form

Objective	Key concepts to consider when addressing the objective	Examples of possible evidence or systems most likely to lead to compliance	Actions to be taken by ILP (if needed)
Competent work practices to avoid **NEGLIGENCE**	Fee earners practice only in areas where they have appropriate competence and expertise.	A written statement setting out the types of matters in which the practice will accept instructions and that instructions will not be accepted in any other types of matters	(Please circle one rating) **NC PC C FC FC Plus**
NEGLIGENCE Objective (Cont'd)	The ambit of the retainer is described precisely in writing to the client and includes a statement of what the practice will do and what the practice will not do.	In every matter there is a written retainer (often part of the costs agreement).	(Please circle one rating) **NC PC C FC FC Plus**
NEGLIGENCE Objective (Cont'd)	The legal practitioner directors meet on a regular basis to review the performance of the practice or, in the case of sole practitioner practices, meetings are held regularly with staff.	Minutes/notes recording the decisions taken at meetings and the actions taken	(Please circle one rating) **NC PC C FC FC Plus**
NEGLIGENCE Objective (Cont'd)	Legal practitioner director/s regularly consider and review workloads, supervision, methods of file review, and communication with clients.	Written records including file registers, number of files assigned to each fee earner, dates and methods of file review	(Please circle one rating) **NC PC C FC FC Plus**
NEGLIGENCE Objective (Cont'd)	Legal practitioner director/s ensure that legal services are always delivered at a consistently high standard.	Up-to-date precedents covering relevant practice areas are available and used, the practice has appropriate resources for legal research in the areas in which it accepts instructions (whether subscriptions to loose leaf services, up to date text books, training in internet based research), and the work of all employed solicitors and paralegals is properly supervised	(Please circle one rating) **NC PC C FC FC Plus**

Self-Assessment Form (Continued)

Objective	Key concepts to consider when addressing the objective	Examples of possible evidence or systems most likely to lead to compliance	Actions to be taken by ILP (if needed)
Effective, timely and courteous **COMMUNICATION**	Clients are always informed in writing of the steps involved in their matter.	Written descriptions of the processes involved in each type of matter in which the practice accepts instructions are available and given to each client. These descriptions can be in the form of a short letter, a brochure, pamphlet, or otherwise.	(Please circle one rating) **NC PC C FC FC Plus**
COMMUNICATION Objective (Cont'd)	The ambit of the retainer is described precisely in writing to the client and includes a statement of what the practice will do and what the practice will not do.	In every matter there is a written retainer (often part of the costs agreement).	(Please circle one rating) **NC PC C FC FC Plus**
COMMUNICATION Objective (Cont'd)	All staff likely to be involved in the matter are disclosed to the client.	Disclosed in retainer and/or costs agreement	(Please circle one rating) **NC PC C FC FC Plus**
COMMUNICATION Objective (Cont'd)	Methods and time frames for communicating with the client are agreed at the start of each matter and are adhered to.	In each matter, a working plan exists which deals, amongst other things, with client communication, including time frames for return of telephone calls, responses to correspondence, responses to emails.	(Please circle one rating) **NC PC C FC FC Plus**
COMMUNICATION Objective (Cont'd)	All comments and complaints by clients are dealt with promptly and, where possible, by someone else in the practice other than the person complained about.	A written record of the system for dealing with client comments and complaints and a written record of monitoring client satisfaction	(Please circle one rating) **NC PC C FC FC Plus**
Timely delivery, review, and follow up of legal services to avoid instances of **DELAY**	The client is regularly kept informed at each stage of the matter and is provided with periodic billing.	A system for ensuring that the working plan in each matter (see above) is adhered to and that the file contains all appropriate file notes or time records or other evidence that the plan has been adhered to	(Please circle one rating) **NC PC C FC FC Plus**

(Continued)

Self-Assessment Form (*Continued*)

Objective	Key concepts to consider when addressing the objective	Examples of possible evidence or systems most likely to lead to compliance	Actions to be taken by ILP (if needed)
DELAY Objective (Cont'd)	The file contains a complete record of all aspects of the transaction or matter.	Copies of all letters, notes, emails, records of telephone calls, statements, calculations, and tax invoices are on file.	(Please circle one rating) **NC PC C FC FC Plus**
DELAY Objective (Cont'd)	Critical dates are recorded, monitored, and complied with.	Procedures for regular review of files, checklists, and a firm-wide diary system, which may or may not be computer based	(Please circle one rating) **NC PC C FC FC Plus**
DELAY Objective (Cont'd)	Procedures for locating files and documents and for monitoring activity in all open files	Documented procedures effective in (a) locating files and tracing documents, correspondence, and other items relating to any matter that is open or has been closed but the file is still retained by the ILP (b) monitoring files for inactivity at predetermined times	(Please circle one rating) **NC PC C FC FC Plus**
Acceptable processes for **LIENS** and **FILE TRANSFERS**	Timely preparation of bills of costs when a file transfer is requested	Policy and procedures covering liens/file transfers, appropriate records of costs to date, and a list of those documents to be transferred or retained where necessary are on file.	(Please circle one rating) **NC PC C FC FC Plus**
LIENS and **FILE TRANSFERS** Objective (Cont'd)	Acceptable processes for release of documents to clients	Rules 14, 15, & 16 covering professional obligations in relation to clients' documents upon termination of retainer are followed subject to § 728 of the Act.	(Please circle one rating) **NC PC C FC FC Plus**
Share understanding & appropriate documentation from commencement through to termination of	The use of established new client engagement procedures including universal use of approved retainer/costs agreements	An acceptable and "client friendly" form of retainer/costs agreement that complies with the Act, the Regulations and the Solicitors' rules	(Please circle one rating) **NC PC C FC FC Plus**

Self-Assessment Form (Continued)

Objective	Key concepts to consider when addressing the objective	Examples of possible evidence or systems most likely to lead to compliance	Actions to be taken by ILP (if needed)
retainer covering **COST DISCLOSURE, BILLING PRACTICES,** and **TERMINATION OF RETAINER**			
COST DISCLOSURE, BILLING PRACTICES, and **TERMINATION OF RETAINER** Objective (Cont'd)	Standardised procedures for collecting client data, opening of new files, and the recording of data within the firm's accounting and practice management systems with provision for separate client records in the case of multi-disciplinary practices	A disclosure policy (e.g., whether or not taking advantage of exceptions to disclosure, policy about disclosure of costs of non-legal services used in the legal matter) with a process ensuring disclosure is made in accordance with the Act, the Regulations, and the Solicitors' Rules. An up-to-date File/Matter Register or Practice Management system listing files and individual client files (complying with Rule 48 as to files and file register).	(Please circle one rating) NC PC C FC FC Plus
COST DISCLOSURE, BILLING PRACTICES, and **TERMINATION OF RETAINER** Objective (Cont'd)	What is to occur when a retainer is terminated and action to be taken if [termination is] to occur close to a critical date.	The client receives written confirmation (unless exceptional circumstances apply) of • the outcome, any further action the client is to take in the matter, and what, if anything, the practice will do next • the arrangements for storage and retrieval of retained documents (if any) • accounting to the client for any outstanding money • return to the client of original documents and other property belonging to the client	(Please circle one rating) NC PC C FC FC Plus

(Continued)

Self-Assessment Form (*Continued*)

Objective	Key concepts to consider when addressing the objective	Examples of possible evidence or systems most likely to lead to compliance	Actions to be taken by ILP (if needed)
		• information about whether the matter should be reviewed in the future and if so, when? Where the practice terminates the retainer or withdraws its services, grounds for such action are clearly stated in writing to the client.	
COST DISCLOSURE, BILLING PRACTICES, and **TERMINATION OF RETAINER** Objective (Cont'd)	Use of an established policy for formulating accounts and a system for checking bills of costs for compliance with policy	Capacity for accurately recording time or another acceptable basis for charging clients and a process for the issue of checked tax invoices to clients	(Please circle one rating) NC PC C FC FC Plus
COST DISCLOSURE, BILLING PRACTICES, and **TERMINATION OF RETAINER** Objective (Cont'd)	Review of all files ready to be closed by legal practitioner director/s or nominated supervising practitioner/s to ensure all steps have been taken to complete the matter, including return of client documents and issue of a final account	Appropriate letter on file, executed releases where needed, provision of copy documents to external parties as required, and a note as to whether client needs further services if new developments arise	(Please circle one rating) NC PC C FC FC Plus
Timely identification and resolution of **CONFLICTS OF INTERESTS,** including when acting for both parties or acting against previous clients as well as potential conflicts that may arise in relationships with debt collectors and mercantile agencies, or conducting another business, referral fees and commissions, etc.	Recognition that • conflicts can emerge in many areas and contexts, be they potential or actual and • conflicts can emerge before or during a retainer, where acting against a previous client, where acting for more than one client, and where the solicitor prefers his/her interests over those of the client	Policy and procedures for conflict of interests checks. The taking of full instructions, especially in commercial matters, from clients as to companies and related entities in which the client is involved. Maintenance of a suitable database that records all relevant details of the parties and related corporation and related entities to facilitate conflict checks	(Please circle one rating) NC PC C FC FC Plus

Self-Assessment Form (Continued)

Objective	Key concepts to consider when addressing the objective	Examples of possible evidence or systems most likely to lead to compliance	Actions to be taken by ILP (if needed)
CONFLICTS OF INTERESTS Objective (Cont'd)	Compliance with Rules 10, 11, 12, 56, and 59	Conflict checks are undertaken prior to file opening and evidence of search processes, including Electronic and paper-based records. When there has been some change in the matter (like a new party becoming involved), further conflict checks are carried out.	(Please circle one rating) **NC PC C FC FC Plus**
CONFLICTS OF INTERESTS Objective (Cont'd)	Being aware of potential conflicts if holding an office that may lead to conflict with the interests of a client	A system for opening and recording files with written policies and procedures and checklists for determining whether a conflict exists	(Please circle one rating) **NC PC C FC FC Plus**
RECORDS MANAGEMENT (minimizing the likelihood of loss or destruction of correspondence and documents through appropriate document retention, filing, archiving, etc., and providing for compliance with requirements regarding registers of files, safe custody, financial interest)	The practice has appropriate mail opening and distribution processes, including electronic mail.	A clear policy and related procedures exist.	(Please circle one rating) **NC PC C FC FC Plus**
RECORDS MANAGEMENT Objective (Cont'd)	File management processes with an appropriate matter closing procedure and a system for safe custody and document retention as well as storing and accessing files	Established processes with checklists for opening, maintaining, moving reviewing, and closing files. Also safe custody/ document retention and file closing records. In	(Please circle one rating) **NC PC C FC FC Plus**

(Continued)

Self-Assessment Form (*Continued*)

Objective	Key concepts to consider when addressing the objective	Examples of possible evidence or systems most likely to lead to compliance	Actions to be taken by ILP (if needed)
		the case of files stored externally, a record of that arrangement. A diary system, which may or may not be computer based, accessible to relevant staff, especially for critical dates in matters. Maintaining a backup record of key dates. Identifying relevant matters (when acting for a client in a number of matters) and linking files (where more than one file is relevant to the client's case).	
RECORDS MANAGEMENT Objective (Cont'd)	Files for legal services are kept separate from files for "nonlegal" services.	A system to determine who is able to access legal files/safe custody and mechanisms to ensure that staff know and observe these.	(Please circle one rating) **NC PC C FC FC Plus**
RECORDS MANAGEMENT Objective (Cont'd)	Compliance with Rules 48, 49, and 50	A File Register, Safe Custody Register, and a Register of Financial Interests are held and are up to date	(Please circle one rating) **NC PC C FC FC Plus**
UNDERTAKINGS (providing for undertakings to be given, monitoring of compliance and timely compliance with notices, orders, rulings, directions, or other requirements of regulatory authorities such as OLSC, Law Society, courts, costs assessors	Knowing the implications of providing undertakings and compliance is monitored on a regular basis.	A register/record of solicitor undertakings (their authorization and monitoring, including discharge) given on behalf of the practice. Timely and full responses are given to notices, orders, rulings, etc.	(Please circle one rating) **NC PC C FC FC Plus**

Self-Assessment Form (*Continued*)

Objective	Key concepts to consider when addressing the objective	Examples of possible evidence or systems most likely to lead to compliance	Actions to be taken by ILP (if needed)
SUPERVISION OF PRACTICE AND STAFF (providing for compliance with statutory obligations covering license and practicing certificate conditions, employment of staff, and ensuring proper quality assurance of work outputs; and performance of legal, paralegal, and non-legal staff involved in the delivery of legal services)	Ensuring all practitioners have practicing certificates and that all legal practitioner directors have unrestricted practicing certificates	Each legal practitioner director must hold an unrestricted practicing certificate and there is to be a record of the appointment of the legal practitioner director.	(Please circle one rating) NC PC C FC FC Plus
SUPERVISION OF PRACTICE AND STAFF Objective (Cont'd)	Ensuring notifications of changes are provided to the Law Society, e.g., new legal practitioner director/s or employed solicitors, etc.	Copies of letter/advices sent to the Law Society of NSW are held.	(Please circle one rating) NC PC C FC FC Plus
SUPERVISION OF PRACTICE AND STAFF Objective (Cont'd)	Legal practitioner directors meet on a regular basis (at least monthly) to review the performance of the practice with an agenda covering such items as operational and work/risk management policies and controls, compliance issues, and people management. In practices with one legal practitioner director, such meetings should be held with senior staff such as selected employed solicitors, paralegals, bookkeeper, etc.	Minutes/notes of such meetings, recording the matters covered, decisions agreed on, and action taken	(Please circle one rating) NC PC C FC FC Plus

(Continued)

Self-Assessment Form *(Continued)*

Objective	Key concepts to consider when addressing the objective	Examples of possible evidence or systems most likely to lead to compliance	Actions to be taken by ILP (if needed)
SUPERVISION OF PRACTICE AND STAFF Objective (Cont'd)	Compliance with the Act, the Regulations, the Solicitors' Rules, and other statutory/taxation obligations	On a periodic basis, at least several times a year, there is a review of compliance. All personnel, both professional and support, are aware of relevant obligations and compliance standards and a record kept of outcomes and action taken. Evidence of compliance with withholding tax obligations, e.g., PAYG, GST, as well as payment of superannuation guarantee contributions	(Please circle one rating) NC PC C FC FC Plus
SUPERVISION OF PRACTICE AND STAFF Objective (Cont'd)	A delegation process ensuring that • staff are clear about the boundaries of their role, responsibilities, and authority • staff are capable of doing the work delegated	People management policies and procedures, a file of executed employment agreements, duty statements/job descriptions of all staff and copies of up to date practicing certificates	(Please circle one rating) NC PC C FC FC Plus
SUPERVISION OF PRACTICE AND STAFF Objective (Cont'd)	A structured induction and training program, which will ensure that all staff are properly trained and qualified for the duties they are employed to perform. Induction and training should also cover statutory obligations in the Legal Profession Act, Privacy, OH&S, Workers Compensation, holidays and leave, etc.	Documented induction procedures for both professional and support staff; a training register for both professional and nonprofessional staff, and records of training needs being addressed in the staff performance review process	(Please circle one rating) NC PC C FC FC Plus
SUPERVISION OF PRACTICE AND STAFF Objective (Cont'd)	Staff performance reviews should be carried out on a periodic basis no less frequently than once a year	Records of regular staff feedback and appraisal	(Please circle one rating) NC PC C FC FC Plus

Self-Assessment Form (Continued)

Objective	Key concepts to consider when addressing the objective	Examples of possible evidence or systems most likely to lead to compliance	Actions to be taken by ILP (if needed)
SUPERVISION OF PRACTICE AND STAFF Objective (Cont'd)	All current files are reviewed by a legal practitioner director or nominated supervising practitioner on an appropriate periodic basis	Notations on files used to review and discuss files with employed solicitors Compliance with policy and procedures is part of staff performance reviews	(Please circle one rating) **NC PC C FC FC Plus**
SUPERVISION OF PRACTICE AND STAFF Objective (Cont'd)	Development of budgets	Budgets are in place and future profitability is monitored.	(Please circle one rating) **NC PC C FC FC Plus**
Avoiding failure to account and breach of Part 3.1 Division 2 of the Act **(TRUST ACCOUNTS)**	Accounting systems established for • General/other • Trust • Controlled money • Transit money	A suitable accounting software package with appropriate written delegations and procedures for the handling of trust monies especially issue of trust account cheques	(Please circle one rating) **NC PC C FC FC Plus**
TRUST ACCOUNTS Objective (Cont'd)	Suitably trained/qualified staff are involved.	Accounting records are accurate, up-to-date and regularly monitored.	(Please circle one rating) **NC PC C FC FC Plus**

Self-assessment completed

Name of ILP _____

Names of staff involved in self-assessment

_____

_____

_____

Certified by _____   **(Legal Practitioner Director)**

_____   **(Legal Practitioner Director)**

NOTES

1. Christine E. Parker, Tahlia Grodon & Steve A. Mark, *Regulating Law Firm Ethics Management: An Empirical Assessment of the Regulation of Incorporated Legal Practices in NSW*, 37 J.L. Soc'y 466.

2. *See id.* at 488.

3. *See* Susan Saab Fortney, *The Role of Ethics Audits in Improving Management Systems and Practices: An Empirical Examination of Management-Based Regulation of Law Firms*, 4 St. Mary's L.J. Symp. Legal Malpractice & Ethics 112, 148 (2014).

4. Ted Schneyer, *Professional Discipline in Law Firms*, 77 Cornell L. Rev. 1 (1991). Professor Schneyer has updated his work; see Ted Schneyer, *The Case for Proactive Management-Based Regulation to Improve Professional Self-Regulation for U.S. Lawyers*, 42 Hofstra L. Rev. 233 (2013).

5. Fortney, *supra* note 3, at 148.

CHAPTER 3

The Main Elements of Risk Management for Lawyers: Understanding When They Are in Place (and When They Are Missing)

To understand what is involved in effective risk management, we must first try to define what constitutes good health in the context of law firm practice and management generally. This requires an understanding of risk management as a continuous process.

Effective risk management has three elements:

1. Identifying risk management categories (encompassing both firm management and practice oversight categories).
2. Knowing what, if any, procedures or systems are already in place in each of the risk management categories.
3. Developing strategies to control risk categories, or particular risks identified but not yet adequately managed.

The first element requires the establishment of a framework of general, if not universal, application among law firms to be used in evaluating risks. The second element, particular to each firm willing to engage in appropriate self-examination, involves active inquiry and investigation to determine the nature and scope of risk management practices that are currently in place. The third element involves posing, for each risk identified during the investigation phase, the question, "What realistic risk management tools could be put in place that would effectively and efficiently control that risk?"

If, for example, a firm has concerns about its ability to catch conflicts of interest at the client intake stage, the firm will need to review both its management structure and its system of file opening, internal notification, and checking for conflicts. Similarly, if a firm notes that a pattern of billing disputes with clients is developing, perhaps involving a particular practice group, it will need to review two aspects of its operations: its engagement letters and its billing policies and procedures. In each case, once the review is complete, the firm can add procedures that may be necessary to remedy any deficiencies that may have been uncovered.

This process, and the list of components of a comprehensive risk management system, may be daunting when viewed as an apparently monolithic structure in the form described here, but it is really just a matter of taking things one step at a time. Precisely because risk management is a process, it does not have to happen (and generally cannot happen) all at once. Both the investigation and implementation elements of the process can, and should, be done in discrete stages and over time. Establishing effective risk management can best be viewed as steady, continuous progress along a defined path, rather than the sudden and jarring imposition of particular (and painful) solutions. To use a medical analogy, risk management should be like taking vitamins, not undergoing major surgery.

The second and third elements of the process previously listed are addressed in later chapters. Part 2 of this book is divided into questionnaires that make it easy for firms to address specific risk management categories separately and according to their own schedule.

When deciding which risk categories are most relevant to its particular needs, a firm should first consider the range of risk management issues. Then the firm can begin the process of evaluation on a selective basis. Likewise, we first turn to a survey of the basic risk management categories.

IDENTIFYING THE RISK MANAGEMENT CATEGORIES

Law Firm Management Structure and the Firm Culture: The Leadership Component in the Control of Risk

Effective risk management within the practice of law can occur only within a management environment that meets two basic requirements:

1. *Authority.* The firm's management must have sufficient authority delegated by all partners to be able to control the practice of all the individual members of the firm without exception (and regardless of seniority) where management perceives the need to impose such controls.
2. *Leadership.* The firm's management must recognize and accept the importance of effective risk management and must actively, continuously, and consistently communicate to all the firm's personnel its commitment to implement risk management throughout the firm.

Assigning the Risk Management Responsibilities

Apart from the requirement that firms recognize the need for effective management is the actual assignment of management functions. To move from the philosophical and cultural recognition of the importance of risk management to its effective introduction throughout the organization, the firm must, in a coherent and centralized way, delegate ongoing duties to control the categories of risk identified as concerns. As discussed previously, this process of moving from the theoretical to the practical requires that a specific partner be designated as general counsel or, at a minimum, that an ethics or risk management committee be given the responsibility and authority to fulfill the day-to-day functions of managing the practice to reduce risk.

Once a firm has recognized the need for loss prevention and delegated the risk management function, it must assess the ways in which the risk categories are relevant to its membership structure, culture, and practice areas. What follows is an outline of the principal risk categories that firms need to manage in today's environment. It cannot be comprehensive, because new risks continue to arise from the practice of law. Nevertheless, it does categorize most of the problems firms have faced since the late 1990s, as liability to clients, third parties, and regulators has become a regular and increasingly serious matter of concern.

The Practice Oversight Categories

The following outline shows the main categories of risk management evaluation. The outline indicates the scope of the risk management function and the necessary reach of any survey that seeks to measure the level of a firm's adoption of risk management principles. Next to the heading of each category is a reference to the relevant questionnaire in part 2 of this book that, together with the corresponding answer and analysis sheet in part 3, explores each subject area in greater depth. For completeness, the first section of the outline reviews the law firm management components just discussed, and the remaining sections encompass the practice oversight components. As mentioned earlier, references to the questionnaires should not be taken as an indication that every risk management topic is of equal concern to every law firm or that firms must address every topic at once to practice appropriate risk management. Rather, the outline is like a complete menu in a restaurant or a list of all medicines available to a physician; firms will choose segments relevant to their own needs, and few will have sufficient appetite to digest the whole subject at one sitting or be ill enough to need the entire pharmacopoeia at once.

I.   **Management Structure**—Questionnaire 1 (see page 59)
       A. Is there a written partnership or shareholder agreement?
              1. Has it been reviewed recently?
              2. Review management and compensation structure to determine whether it may unduly reward client introduction or other competitive behavior that is likely to impede management.
       B. Review management structure generally and
              1. Determine whether adequate personnel and time are allocated to management.
              2. Determine whether management functions are adequately compensated to encourage appropriate time and energy to be devoted to managing the firm.

II. **Risk Management Oversight**—Questionnaire 2 (see page 61)
   A. Who is responsible for risk management oversight, and what is that person's (or committee's) title?
   B. What is the scope of the risk management function, and what is included within or excluded from the function?
   C. Does the person or committee have sufficient authority, time, staff, and resources to perform this function?
   D. Are partners, professionals, and support staff trained in and aware of the risk management structure, the chain of responsibility and authority, and their individual responsibilities to report every kind of issue and concern to the responsible person?
   E. What is the nature and scope of the protocol for training and ongoing dissemination of risk management policies and procedures at every level in the firm?
   F. Does the firm have policies and procedures for controlling lawyers' freedom of access to the media?
   G. Does the firm have programs to deal with alcohol, drug, and stress-related problems?
   H. Does the firm have training, Continuing Legal Education (CLE), and development policies and practices?
      1. Review policies and procedures regarding in-house and outside CLE, including monitoring compliance with state bar requirements.
      2. Review policies and procedures for disseminating and conveying importance of risk management policies and procedures throughout the firm other than mere circulation of policy manuals, including the following:
         a. use of in-house seminars, retreats, and lunch meetings
         b. knowledge of policies and procedures generally
   I. Does the firm have internal reporting policies and procedures?
      1. Confirm existence of, and review policies and procedures for, internal reporting, including violations of any risk management policy or procedure, or any other ethical problems.
      2. Review policies for handling all reports of such occurrences, including identification and availability of
         a. internal general counsel
         b. external ethics counsel or equivalent
         c. appropriate protection of whistle-blowers
      3. Review knowledge among partners and all professional staff of reporting policies and procedures.
      4. Confirm that the exercise of the risk management function is combined with sufficient authority to address such occurrences.
      5. Review policies and procedures regarding fee disputes, fee collections, and independent assessment of whether to commence suit for fees. (Note: This is a cross-check on the matters covered by Questionnaire 4.)
   J. Does the firm have response procedures?
      1. Insurers
         a. Confirm familiarity with insurance policy requirements, law of disclaimers, and procedures for compliance.

      b. Review files relating to all incidents reported to insurers within three years before current review; check for

        (1) timeliness of notification

        (2) adequacy of notification

        (3) adequacy of cooperation with insurer or assigned counsel

  2. Clients

      a. Review policies and procedures for notifying clients of incidents constituting potential claims.

      b. Review procedures for assigning partner to deal with matters involving actual or potential problems, including dealings with courts, opposing counsel, and any replacement counsel.

      c. Check files involving all incidents reported to clients within three years before current evaluation for compliance with policies and procedures.

  3. Professional Authorities

      a. Review policies and procedures for reporting current violations of rules of professional conduct to appropriate authorities (both for violations arising inside the firm and those noted in dealings with opposing counsel).

      b. Review all files relating to such reports made within three years before current evaluation.

  4. Public Relations

      a. Review policies and procedures for assigning one spokesperson, and for determining responses to media enquiries, including review of policies of any outside consultants.

      b. Review public relations responses as well as press and media coverage regarding all incidents in three years before current evaluation.

K. Professional Liability Coverage Management

  1. Review existing policies with broker; check for

      a. level of coverage and deductible

      b. per-lawyer premiums

      c. special provisions or exclusions

      d. coverage of all areas of firm's practice

      e. disclaimer provisions

  2. Confirm that risk management partner or committee is responsible for coverage issues.

  3. Confirm review by risk management partner within prior year.

  4. Review potential for negotiating premium, and review deductible level.

L. General Counsel and Other Internal Review Structures

  1. Delineate role of existing general counsel.

  2. Delineate risk management areas not encompassed by general counsel's responsibilities.

  3. Review reporting structure, hierarchy, and utilization by lawyers and professional staff of general counsel.

     4. Review concerns and issues raised by general counsel.
     5. Review concerns and issues raised by personnel administrators.
     6. Review sufficiency of resources critical to general counsel.

III. **New Client/Matter Intake**—Questionnaire 3 (see page 65)

    A. New Business Screening and Intake

      1. Who is responsible for oversight and implementation of the intake process?

      2. Can the introducing lawyer unilaterally make client selection decisions?

      3. What screening mechanisms are in place, and how is information gathered and distributed in connection with new client and new matter acceptance?

    B. Conflicts

      1. Identification and Analysis of Conflicts

        a. Review all information forms for new and prospective clients; determine whether, when properly used, the forms will identify

          (1) conflicts between or among existing and/or former clients of the firm and clients of individual lawyers who have joined laterally, as well as staff (such as secretaries and legal assistants) with access to confidential information

          (2) entrepreneurial activities and other personal-interest conflicts involving lawyers, staff, and prospective clients

          (3) "positional" or issue conflicts

          (4) conflicts of temporary or contract lawyers and staff

        b. Review all systems and procedures for collection and distribution of new client forms and for scope of information required.

        c. Review procedures used by administrative staff in checking for conflicts.

        d. Review policies and procedures for firm management oversight regarding (1) client acceptance and (2) disclosure decisions when actual or potential conflicts are identified.

        e. Review policies and procedures for engaging in "beauty contests."

          (1) Review prior discussion of potential conflict with potential clients.

          (2) Within the firm, review the adequacy of the process used to obtain any required prior approvals.

      2. Waivers and Consents

        a. Review standard form letters or procedure for preparing and issuing client-specific letters, requesting client consent to act where potential conflict exists, including appropriate disclosure language.

        b. Review procedures for ensuring use of standard form, or for obtaining a variance or specially prepared letters, where potential conflicts have been identified.

    c. Review sample files to determine whether waivers based on adequate disclosure were actually obtained.

3. Oversight, Control, and Avoidance
   a. Review claims of conflicts in the three years before current audit.
   b. Review partners' and professional staff's knowledge of and compliance with policies and procedures for
      (1) conflicts checking
      (2) use of new client forms
      (3) obtaining exceptions, if any
      (4) prenotification of participation in beauty contests
      (5) adequate disclosure and use of standard form or client-specific letters regarding waivers
   c. Review policies and procedures for monitoring changes in client composition (e.g., changes in corporate structure, change in status of client, substitution of client in same matter).
   d. Review policies and procedures for restarting or completing conflicts-checking process when client composition changes.
   e. Review partners' and professional staff's knowledge of and compliance with these policies and procedures.

C. Ability to Pay Appropriate Fees and Business Suitability
   1. Review fee arrangement in light of anticipated work.
   2. Review client's ability to pay.
   3. Review suitability of retainer terms and arrangements.
   4. Confirm absence of prior history of nonpayment or significant accounts receivable.
   5. Confirm absence of "business" conflicts.

D. Assignment of Personnel
   1. Review procedures for identifying nature of client problem.
   2. Confirm existence of oversight procedure independent of introducing partner.
   3. Review procedures for convening meetings and making decisions.
   4. Control overstaffing by
      a. reviewing authority of oversight partner or committee, and level of adherence to decisions regarding partners' assignments
      b. reviewing policies and procedures for assigning professional staff, including use of existing skills versus retraining partners' preassigned staff
      c. reviewing policies and procedures for avoiding overcommitment of staff to given matter (i.e., minimizing potential for overbilling), and overcommitment of individuals (i.e., taking on too much work in time available, with potential for inadequate work product)

E. Engagement and Nonengagement Letters
   1. Confirm requirement to use engagement letters for new clients, scope of engagement confirmations for new matters for existing clients, and nonengagement letters where initial

contact does not result in engagement, including following beauty contests.

2. Confirm existence of requirement that new clients counter-sign engagement letters.

3. Confirm existence of review procedures to ensure compliance with engagement letter and nonengagement letter requirements, including actual receipt of countersigned engagement letters.

4. Review use of and departure from standard forms as follows:
   a. Review use of standard form engagement and nonengagement letters.
   b. Review policies and procedures for varying standard forms and arrangements.

5. Review procedures to determine whether policies and procedures are being adhered to for both engagement and nonengagement letters.

F. Terms of Engagement

1. Review policies regarding the following:
   a. nonrefundable and other inappropriate fee arrangements
   b. entrepreneurial arrangements of any type with clients
   c. authority to terminate client relationships

2. Review policies regarding client-provided guidelines.

3. Review knowledge of the partners, professional staff, and clerical staff regarding all of these policies and procedures.

IV. **Client Relations, Fees, Billing, and Collections**—Questionnaire 4 (see page 71)

A. Confidentiality

1. Review policies and procedures for ensuring protection of client confidences, including controls and protections regarding
   (a) public display of files, papers
   (b) outsider access to lawyers' offices and support areas
   (c) use of e-mail and other electronic communications technologies

2. Review knowledge of lawyers and professional staff regarding these policies and controls, including scope of training and dissemination of the information.
   a. Review compliance with these policies and controls.
   b. Review policies and procedures for communicating confidentiality-protection issues to and obtaining appropriate instructions from clients.

B. Client Communications

1. Review existence and scope of requirements for regular communication with clients.

2. Review procedures for obtaining client feedback regarding quality of services provided.

C. Billing and Collections

1. Review policies and procedures for time recording and entry and confirm degree of compliance.

2. Review existence, scope, and degree of enforcement of controls over unauthorized, nonstandard, or otherwise improper billing practices.

D. Collection Procedures
   1. Confirm that collection partners cannot unilaterally write off substantial receivables and that appropriate criteria are used for making write-off decisions.
   2. Review all significant outstanding receivables at least yearly.
   3. Review policies and procedures for collecting overdue bills and suing clients, including matter reviews and the decision-making process before commencing a suit.

E. Client/Matter Closing Letters
   1. Confirm existence of, and review policy requiring issuance of, client/matter closing letters at end of engagement (or new engagement letters, for which the firm accepts continuing review obligations).
   2. Review standard forms; check for language stating that no follow-up work will be performed, and no client notification of changes in law will be provided, without a new engagement letter.
   3. Review lawyers' and professional staff's knowledge of the need for, and policies regarding the use of, closing letters.
   4. Review policies and procedures for compliance (e.g., reminders or billing-system fail-safe requirements).
   5. Check a random sample of files to confirm compliance.

V. **Docket (Tickler or Critical Date Reminder) and Calendar Systems**—Questionnaire 5 (see page 75)

A. Calendar and Docket Systems
   1. Is there a central calendaring system for firm, offices, or practice groups?
   2. Are there any lawyers, groups, or offices with no central, and only personal, calendars?
   3. To the extent there is any central calendaring, are lawyers permitted to maintain personal and individual calendars?
   4. Where there are central calendars, who is responsible for overseeing them?
   5. To what extent is the firm using available technology to force central, and prevent individual, calendaring and docket control?
   6. How comprehensive are the central systems in various special practice areas (e.g., litigation, tax, intellectual property, and regulatory)?
   7. How comprehensive is the reminder system, and does it work effectively to prevent missed deadlines and unnecessary last-minute rush projects in each practice area?

B. File Controls
   1. Review systems and controls on issuance of file numbers.
   2. Review systems and controls for locating and storing "live" and "dead" files.

      3. Review systems and controls for inventory, storage, and location of original documents.

      4. Review systems and controls for backup and storage of computer memory:

         a. for client/matter/form/library materials

         b. for administrative and accounting management materials

      5. Review policies and procedures for retention and destruction of dead files.

      6. Review policies and procedures for files created or modified on laptops, personal smartphones, tablets, and home computers.

C. Closing Letters

      1. Is a policy in place for sending closing letters when matters are concluded?

      2. Is a standard form provided?

      3. Are monitoring procedures in place to trigger closing letters (or obtain management approval for an exception) when matters are dormant and unbilled for a fixed amount of time?

VI. **Practice and Human Resource Management**—Questionnaire 6 (see page 79)

A. New Employee Orientation

      1. Are there formal orientation programs for all new lawyer and nonlawyer hires at every level of the firm?

      2. What topics are addressed?

      3. Does the orientation include a thorough review of the firm's risk management policies?

B. Practice Management

      1. Review the nature, structure, and composition of practice groups.

         a. Are matters assigned to individuals or practice groups?

         b. Are there practice areas in which only one attorney has expertise?

         c. Explore whether—and if so, to what extent—matters are handled from beginning to end by a single lawyer.

      2. Review policies and procedures for frequency and effectiveness of oversight of all lawyers' work.

      3. Review policies and procedures for identifying lawyers with any kind of practice or personal problems; also review policies and procedures for transfer of client responsibilities.

C. Opinion and Audit Letter Issuance

      1. Use of Standard Forms and Client-Specific Letters

         a. Review standard form letters.

         b. Review policies and procedures for signing and issuing all opinions and letters, including independent review or second-signature requirement.

         c. Review procedures for monitoring changes in the substantive law of third-party liability for opinion and auditor letters.

         d. Review policies and procedures for updating standard forms to conform to substantive law developments.

2. Procedures for Variances
    a. Review policies and procedures for independent review and signing of letters with variances from standard forms.
    b. Review knowledge of partners and professional staff regarding risk management policies and procedures governing opinion and audit letters.
3. Control over Compliance
    a. Review procedures to monitor compliance with use of standard forms, issuance or second-signature requirements, and independent review of variances.
    b. Check a random sample of files containing opinion or audit letters to confirm compliance with policies and procedures.
D. Continuous Practice Review
    1. Review detailed procedure and documentation, including questionnaires and reporting material relating to periodic review of the work of all partners.
    2. Confirm that the review process is being conducted regularly, and check files relating to recent sample reviews.
E. Branch Office Controls
    1. Review policies and procedures for monitoring compliance by branch offices with all risk management functions, policies, and procedures.
    2. Review knowledge of branch office partners and professional staff of all risk management policies and procedures, and compare to those policies and procedures used at the home office.
    3. Conduct checks at branch offices parallel to all those conducted at the home office, and compare compliance.
F. Lateral Partner and Merged Practice Controls
    1. Confirm prehiring and merger risk management checks being performed.
    2. Confirm client intake policies and procedures being strictly followed before new client matters are opened.
    3. Confirm existence of effective orientation process to train and inform merging practices and lateral hires in the firm's risk management policies and procedures.
G. Oversight Policies and Practices
    1. Review supervision, review, and evaluation policies as follows:
        a. Review policies and procedures for regular review of all nonpartner professional and support staff.
        b. Review policies and procedures for review by professional staff of supervisors and partners.
        c. Review grievance policies and procedures.
        d. Obtain partner and professional staff evaluations of workings of these oversight and review policies and procedures.
        e. Review compensation structure for professional personnel, availability of family leave, flexible hours, and quality-of-life programs.

          f. Review policies and procedures to ensure compliance with laws and court rules relating to attorney registration or required bar association membership.

      2. Review hiring processes; check for

          a. reference checks and transcript validation

          b. written interview policies

      3. Review termination processes; check for

          a. counseling process

          b. documentation of reviews

          c. compliance with written policies

          d. independent prior review of terminations

          e. restriction of access to electronic documents and return of mobile devices

      4. Review controls and procedures for impaired personnel as follows:

          a. Review policies and procedures for periodic enquiry to find and evaluate changes in partner and professional personnel behavior.

          b. Review policies and procedures for encouraging early reporting of and counseling for impairment problems.

          c. Review written questionnaires and materials regularly circulated regarding impairment.

          d. Confirm regular compliance with impairment review policies.

          e. Review contact between firm and bar association or insurer impairment programs.

      5. Review antidiscrimination policies and procedures as follows:

          a. Review written policies.

          b. Review frequency of distribution.

          c. Review procedures for handling complaints and problems.

          d. Review knowledge of policies:

             (1) within the firm generally

             (2) among those responsible for human resource matters, including those handling complaints and problems

   H. Review of Policies Regarding Succession Planning and Lawyer Transitions

VII. Trust Accounts and Financial Controls—Questionnaire 7 (see page 85)

   A. Review escrow account records for three years before current evaluation and verify complete compliance with applicable rules of professional conduct.

   B. Check that all deviations from applicable rules of professional conduct were reported to disciplinary authorities if required.

   C. Review all escrow and client account policies and procedures to determine adequacy to assure continued compliance with applicable rules of professional conduct.

   D. Review all policies and procedures for reimbursing expenses and for charging clients for expenses.

   E. Review policies and procedures for overseeing compliance with billing policies and procedures.
   F. Confirm firm accounts are regularly audited and that auditors have reviewed the firm's financial controls.
VIII. **Technology and Data Security Systems**—Questionnaire 8 (see page 87)
   A. Review management structure and policies and procedures for storing and protecting digital data.
   B. Review policies and practices for training with respect to data security
   C. Review policies and practices regarding personal use of firm software and hardware.
   D. Review policies and procedures in the event of data breaches.
   E. Review policies for bringing your own device.
   F. Review policies and procedures for social networking usage, both generally and in research.
   G. Review data retention and destruction policies and procedures.
   H. Review use of cloud computing.
   I. Review policies for file backup and recovery in the event of temporary restrictions on access to data or temporary or permanent data loss.
IX. **Non-Technology-Related Disaster Recovery Planning**—Questionnaire 9 (see page 89)
   A. Impact Analysis
      1. Review level of planning for a disaster:
         a. plan preparation and maintenance
         b. frequency of review
         c. distribution arrangements
         d. identification of emergency recovery site
         e. equipment availability
         f. roles of personnel in event of a disaster
         g. identification and training of a recovery team
         h. service and utility availability and arrangements
         i. contact list and arrangements
      2. Review operation of support functions:
         a. role of support staff
         b. availability of supplies
         c. availability of backed-up data and software necessary for practice and essential support functions
      3. Review storage and availability of backup records necessary for continuing practice.
   B. Response Procedures
      1. Maintenance of calendar, time, and docket control functions.
      2. Review of plan by risk managers.
      3. Adequacy of notification arrangements to personnel, clients, and other affected parties.
      4. Adequacy of composition of the recovery team.
      5. Procedures in event of sudden death or incapacity of professionals.

This framework for evaluating risk management is not exhaustive. For instance, categories could be added that relate to specific practice areas or particular activities that lawyers often undertake. Nevertheless, this outline sets the firm on the road to understanding what risk management includes.

IDENTIFYING RISK MANAGEMENT ALREADY IN PLACE

Two elements that help determine which components of risk management are actually in place within a firm are often in conflict:

1. what the firm's management *thinks* is in place, based on policy manuals and procedures, firm "culture," or specific directives, and
2. what the people practicing law within the firm actually *do* on a day-to-day basis, including partners, associates, and support staff

Policies that a firm's management thinks are in place can be totally different from what the firm's lawyers actually do on a daily basis, and this variation can occur in every one of the risk management categories described above. As to any given policy, if the firm does not have in place a verification system or procedure, the odds are great that at least some of the lawyers are avoiding or evading the policy. The deviation between theory and actual practice can be trivial, or it can go to the heart of the firm's risk profile. But ascertaining the scope of the disconnect between theory and practice in any given firm is central to the risk management audit.

To repeat: Whether it is accessible on the web or printed on premium stock and placed in an impressive binder, the most elegant and beautifully written policy manual in the world is meaningless if it is ignored.[1] In fact, the failure to follow a recognized policy can itself have adverse consequences such as damages or disciplinary litigation. Put another way, there must be more than just an initial, one-time announcement or circulation of policies. There must also be provision for a continuing initiation of newcomers and for appropriate reminders to both lawyers and nonlawyers of the content and significance of firm-critical policies.

With the increasingly detailed questionnaires that comprise their application forms, professional liability insurers try to compel at least parts of this verification process. Unfortunately, the attention these questionnaires receive is often perfunctory at best, and the opportunity for an effective review of management practices is lost for another year. Without continuous monitoring from the perspectives of both management and staff, even adequate risk management policies may be useless. To await initiation or completion of the insurance application process, which might not even ask a question that would require the relevant review, might allow more than enough time for a breakdown in the risk management system to occur. Such a delay might also allow time for circumstances to develop that will lead to a claim. The best policies have verification systems built in. For instance, the latest software for managing client intake enables firms to verify every element of the prospective engagement including, for instance, whether an approved engagement letter has been sent to and countersigned by the client.

Chapters 2 through 4 explain the role of law firm audits in enabling firms to take control of the process of determining what level of risk management is in place and where the gaps are. A firm interested in performing an audit will then have all the background necessary to proceed to the questionnaires in part 2 of this book. Part 3 will then reveal, question by question, what each answer indicates regarding the state of the firm's risk management.

DEVELOPING ADEQUATE RISK MANAGEMENT

Assuming that the firm's management has recognized the need to adopt effective risk management strategies, and assuming that a survey has therefore been done to verify the systems already in place, the firm must turn to developing and implementing new policies and procedures. As expressed by one firm's general counsel, "The standard reaction is, 'Don't bother me; I'm not your problem; go bother Joe down the hall—he had the last claim.'" Furthermore, many lawyers who are accustomed to billing by the hour resent bitterly (though not necessarily wisely) any new procedure that arguably "wastes" billable time on apparently non-income-producing activities. Not surprisingly, our view is that over time, such an approach generally creates unnecessary risks of mortgaging or destroying the future in order to avoid implementing relatively modest risk management practices in the present. If a risk management program is well conceived, its burdens should be small compared to its benefits. If the burdens appear to outweigh the benefits, the first approach should be to look for more appropriate policies—not simply to ignore a risk or hope that the firm's past luck continues to hold until after particular lawyers have retired and any applicable statutes of limitation have run their course.

Risk management controls should generally be self-executing to the extent practicable. "Self-executing" means that the control works as an automatic alert and that if an automatic control fails, the activity cannot proceed. A simple example is a file-opening system with a procedure in place whereby, before a file can be opened, a copy of the engagement letter sent to the client (or, even more useful, already countersigned by the client) must be submitted to a designated administrator. Similarly, many firms require that no time be recorded as billable until all mandated conflicts checking, engagement letters, and assignment of staff decisions and processes have been completed and the required independent approvals given. In this way, the incentive on the partner and staff is to comply—quickly and efficiently—with the systems.

The importance of this kind of control is clear from the example of a New York firm that was allowed to proceed with a suit against one of its lawyers, who had solicited a client to pay him individually in return for a limitation of the firm's bill.[2] If controls had been in place, the lawyer would have known that as soon as the billing process began, his attempt to redirect payment would have been detected.

Some procedures or controls are, by their nature, only partly self-executing. For example, in many firms, formal opinion letters require the signature of two partners (this is done to ensure oversight of documents likely to be asserted as a basis for liability against the firm). Such a policy works only if the attorney who is asked to prepare such a letter initially complies with the policy by showing a draft to the appropriate partner or committee. Nevertheless, there may be room for additional controls to increase the likelihood of compliance. In many if not most cases, the actual or potential need for such a letter will be apparent from the time the matter is opened. If new-matter forms require that such a possibility be identified, the appropriate second signer can be identified from the outset—and perhaps before the opportunity or urge to subvert the policy arises. Many firms with tax opinion practices, for example, establish the second-opinion process at the outset to assure compliance with IRS Circular 230.

Whether intended to be self-executing or not, a second element of any system of controls must also be present: "the Rule of Law." In other words, and subject only to such express exceptions as are (wisely) contained in a firm's policies, no one can be above the firm's "law" or allowed to flout it. No matter how senior or venerated, or how large the billings of a partner or practice group, everyone must be subject to the same basic rules and procedures. In other words, there may be policies that are specially adapted to the practical or legal needs of a particular practice area, such as the need of tax lawyers to comply with IRS Circular 230 and the need of securities lawyers to comply with Sarbanes-Oxley requirements. Beyond principled and reasonable exceptions such as these, however, the firm's rules and procedures must be applied—and must be perceived to be applied—consistently.

NOTES

1. For a more thorough discussion of office manuals, see Howard I. Hatoff & Robert C. Wert, Law Office Policy & Procedures Manual (ABA Law Practice Management Section, 5th ed. 2006).
2. Butler, Fitzgerald & Potter v. Beggans, No. 93 Civ. 2588 (S.D.N.Y. Aug. 23, 1994).

CHAPTER 4

Identifying Risk: The Role of Law Firm Audits and Assessments

The first element of risk management is to identify the nature and scope of the risks facing law firms—and whether they have in place effective (or any) tools designed to manage those risks. Only when a firm has taken stock can it enhance—or create from scratch—the policies, procedures, and systems that are appropriate to manage those risks. To that end, this chapter addresses in greater depth why law firms need to consider periodic risk management audits or assessments. The questionnaires that form the basis of such an assessment follow, tracking the sequence of topics outlined in chapter 3. For each questionnaire there is an answer and analysis chart that explains the significance and implications of each of the questions posed. Chapter 5 then discusses how firms can best approach the task of enhancing existing risk management tools or developing new ones that will work, taking into account the varied cultures of large law firms. The goal is to develop strategies to implement the findings of a risk assessment or audit in a way that is constructive, positive, efficient, and as sensitive as possible to the need to minimize unnecessary administrative chores. For guidance on how to conduct audits using the questionnaires, consult the appendix.

THE FUNDAMENTAL PURPOSE OF AUDIT ASSESSMENTS

The following quotation from Demosthenes, for which the authors are indebted to Professor Donald Langevoort,[1] precisely encapsulates the argument for using audits as an essential ingredient of modern risk management: "Nothing is easier than self-deceit. For what each man wishes, that he also believes to be true."[2] This quotation highlights two aspects of the problem facing the legal profession today. As described in chapter 1, despite massive claims, settlements, and judgments against the most prestigious firms, and despite the growing influence of law firm general counsel in most firms, there is still far too much denial within law firms that problems exist. And even when risks are recognized, mere lip service to the existence of problems without sustained and meaningful follow-through is of limited utility. Lawyers and firms need to come to grips with the actual and potential dangers facing them, and must then respond appropriately.

The first step, then, is twofold: to identify and confront directly the risks involved in a lawyer's or firm's practice and then to evaluate the existing policies and procedures already in place to control those risks. Without this initial review and analysis, it is impossible to determine what changes are appropriate or how to implement them effectively. Similarly, the best available texts on risk management and the clearest policy manuals will not constitute effective risk management if they are circulated in a vacuum of ignorance or simply lie, unused, on dusty shelves or on portions of firm intranets that are rarely consulted.

A formal audit assessment, on the other hand, forces a firm to deal with risk management. By their nature, audits compel involvement. And to be most effective, audits should be a part of an ongoing process rather than a once-in-a-lifetime event.

While this idea is less revolutionary than when the first edition of this book was published in 1993, it is by no means a commonplace part of law firms' calendars. By contrast, major international accounting firms perform at least some level of risk management audits as a matter of routine. They may carry out annual self-audits on specific practice areas, involving, for instance, reviews of files to check for compliance with relevant policies and procedures. On a regular but less frequent basis, a firm may call in outside auditors to confirm that the firm's policies and procedures meet industry standards and that it is actually conforming to its own requirements.

Interestingly, in at least some spheres, clients are insisting that the law firms they hire demonstrate adherence to the same kinds of guidelines that govern these clients' own operations. This is most common in the sphere of technology. Almost every firm of any substance that serves major corporations—especially in regulated industries such as banking, finance, and health care—is getting used to having to provide answers to audit questionnaires that are significantly more detailed and probing than the more generic questionnaire that addresses those issues here.

But it should not be necessary for lawyers to wait for their clients to force them to address the adequacy of their risk management systems. Precisely to achieve the positive benefits of risk management discussed earlier—and to differentiate themselves from competitors—law firms should regularly assess the different and growing categories of risk they face and look for ways to enhance or develop risk management protocols that will permit them to demonstrate—to themselves as well as to their clients—that they understand their environment and are doing their best to be in control of their destinies.

Because the nature and scale of the risk environment in which law firms exist is continuously expanding, it is increasingly impractical to do global risk management audits and assessments all at one time. Instead, the different risk categories discussed in chapter 3 can be examined separately, and sequentially from time to time, rather than all at once.

Finally, it is worth remembering that risk assessment has been an integral part of the legal landscape since the dawn of lawyering. Practice management is at least as old as the first moment in history when one lawyer asked a colleague to review a potential argument or a draft document, or when a senior lawyer hired a junior lawyer and helped that junior lawyer learn the ropes. The rest is a matter of degree.

ADDITIONAL USES FOR LAW FIRM AUDIT ASSESSMENTS

The risk management audit assessment has significant utility beyond identifying what are increasingly referred to as "enterprise risks" or testing and improving the risk management tools already in place. There are six common additional uses for audits:

1. as a tool to improve firm-wide management structures, especially for firms with offices in multiple locations, time zones, jurisdictions, and cultures
2. as a "due diligence" tool in evaluating prospective merger candidates or in acquiring practice groups from other firms
3. as a way to demonstrate a firm's strengths to its current or prospective clients
4. as a response to claims
5. as a way to demonstrate a firm's strengths to its current or prospective professional liability insurers
6. as an element of professional supervision or discipline

Improving Law Firm Management Structures

The starkest example of the diffuse management structure common in the legal profession is the large law firm with multiple offices spread across national or international borders and often several continents. In these firms, problems that arise from lack of control of diverse practices within firms are multiplied geometrically.[3] Basic issues like conflicts checking are made vastly more complex, and the challenges of maintaining a uniform level of competence and of imposing any central management are greatly increased. For firms with these structures, audits should be a regular tool to help ensure adherence to basic firm management requirements as well as risk management policies. Where firms confront the potential (or in some cases the recent experience) of significant claims against them arising from the activities of an office perhaps thousands of miles from the headquarters office, there is no alternative to the use of ongoing audits if meaningful risk management is to be maintained.

Using Audits as Due Diligence Tools

The difficulties of assessing potential merger candidates' practices before an acquisition, and of actually assimilating the two firms afterward, are enormous. Yet in many instances, lawyers undertake these transactions in the kind of cavalier manner that they would never permit in their clients' commercial dealings. Indeed, the very concept of applying due diligence techniques to transactions among law firms is often ignored.

As every professional liability insurer can attest, this abdication of normal commercial caution has caused many firms to suffer significant losses. Such due diligence audits would encompass elements of risk management deemed critical to the practices of both firms involved in the merger discussions. For instance, firms often review each other's conflicts-checking mechanisms as part of the preliminary conflicts check. From a risk management point of view, this exercise should be extended to all client intake issues. Similarly, it is difficult to deny the importance of conducting reviews of billing practices and systems as well as of calendar and docket controls to avoid potential embarrassments later.

Due diligence audits will, however, do more than disclose potential dangers in the forms of inadequate client intake control or of ineffective calendar or docket management. They will also reveal basic firm "culture" issues, discussed in the introduction and in chapter 1, including the degree to which the need for risk management (or any management) is accepted by the merger candidate or practice group being studied. A firm's willingness—or unwillingness—to undertake an audit may also speak volumes about the degree to which it has already addressed the specific risk management issues of concern to the acquiring firm. As always, if deals are prevented by the application of the audit process, the great likelihood is that they would have been bad deals for the acquiring firm.

Using Audits to Respond to Claims

Professional liability insurers have increasingly recognized the usefulness of audit assessments as mechanisms to identify causes of recent occurrences and as a basis for developing control tools to prevent future claims and losses. The audit is, of course, at least partly an effort to close the barn door after the horse has bolted. Nevertheless, insurers are increasingly requesting risk management audits after a history or pattern of claims has begun to develop, either as a condition of renewal or as an element in calculating the renewal premium. While both the profession and the insurance industry are not yet at the point of making audits an automatic response to claims, this moment may soon arrive.

Insurers have traditionally adopted a variety of ways to deal with firms that have significant claims or loss histories. These include the obvious—increased premiums (which can be selective or across the board) and increased deductibles (or self-insured retentions, as they are sometimes called by insurers). Insurers may also add policy terms and conditions that effectively impose risk management techniques. Within this context, the audit, as a significant tool in the process of determining what insurance coverage is appropriate for particular firms—and at what price—appears to be gaining favor among underwriters.

There is one crucial aspect of audits imposed by insurers in response to claims or losses that distinguishes them from audits undertaken for any other reason, namely, the confidentiality (or the obligation to waive confidentiality) of the findings or report generated by the audit. In the authors' experience, it is usually in the firm's interest to waive confidentiality and provide the report to the insurer, so long as the firm understands that the insurer will use the information to track the firm's progress (or lack thereof). While the outcome of this tension or potential conflict is likely to depend on the relative negotiating power of the firms and the underwriters, firms will benefit from dealing with risk management issues before a crisis arises.

Demonstrating Risk Management Commitment to Clients

Clients in regulated industries often require law firms to undergo very detailed audits, particularly in the sphere of technology and data protection, as a precondition for receiving work. A few firms have turned this practice to their advantage, recognizing a significant marketing value in demonstrating the strength of their risk management systems. In the sphere of technology, it is becoming standard practice for London-based law firms to qualify themselves as ISO/IEC 27001 compliant, and a few U.S.-based firms have begun to follow suit. ISO/IEC 27001 is an international security management standard, and certification includes review by an outside auditor. Other firms have gone further, and developed risk management protocols which they trumpet to their clients and prospects as reasons to engage them. Well-implemented risk management can give law firms a real competitive advantage in the marketplace.

Demonstrating Risk Management Commitment to Malpractice Insurers

A relatively small number of companies offer lawyers' professional liability insurance, and they are increasingly sophisticated in assessing the risks they will assume. As a result, both law firms and their brokers are increasingly turning to law firm audits as a means of demonstrating the firms' current risk management structure and commitment to effective risk management in the future. Any firm that is interested in differentiating itself from similar firms in its insurers' eyes should consider discussing the possible benefits of undergoing a risk management audit with its insurance broker. But firms that do decide to undergo an audit should realize that they are setting a baseline for future evaluation by, and discussion with, their underwriters. Accordingly, an audit should not be viewed as a one-time event to impress an insurer. Rather, it should be undertaken if the firm genuinely wishes to stay the course and use the audit results to continually upgrade its risk management systems, policies, and procedures. If that is indeed the goal, the audit path is well worth pursuing.

Using Audits to Meet Professional Disciplinary Standards

In the small number of states that have the right to impose discipline on law firms, and in all states that have adopted a version of ABA Model Rules 5.1 and 5.3, the existence of at least some systems to guard against errors is non-negotiable. Audits can play an essential part of seeing to it that the firm has in place and employs systems that will pass disciplinary muster.

WHY SELF-AUDITS?

The Goals of a Law Firm Self-Audit

The questionnaires and the answer and analysis sheets in parts 2 and 3 of this book are intended to demystify the risks, resolve the dilemmas, and provide a structure for the analysis and control of risk elements in a law practice. While these materials can be used in an externally supervised audit process, they are designed for use in a self-audit, in which firms complete the following steps:

- Evaluate, in a structured and coherent framework, the state of risk management already in place.
- Determine the nature and scope of changes needed to existing policies and procedures to better control the risks inherent in the firm's practice.
- Make necessary changes in a manner and on a timetable consistent with the firm's management style and dynamics (part of a firm's culture) or, in appropriate circumstances, as a prelude to changing the prevailing culture.
- Justify recognition by the firm's professional liability insurers of the firm's control over its practice, with a view to qualifying for premium savings in the years to come.

Advantages of the "Do-It-Yourself" Approach

Self-audits offer firms an opportunity to follow the maxim of the late Robert McKay, former dean of New York University School of Law:

> Who used to say that if the legal profession failed to regulate itself, others would do it for us

And for many lawyers, doing it yourself—at least at the start—will be far more palatable than airing one's dirty laundry before others. Among other things, a firm that conducts a self-audit can more effectively control the focus and the distribution of any audit findings, the timing of the audit, the costs of the audit, the use to which findings are put, and the degree and timing of any implementation program.

Control over Content and Disclosure. As noted above, it is increasingly likely that firms with poor claims histories will be pressured into undertaking risk management audits and revealing at least in some fashion the findings—or perhaps, minimally, the corrective steps indicated by the findings—of such audits. By undertaking the process ahead of such pressure, firms may be able to retain much greater freedom about what, if anything, to reveal. Alternatively, firms may be sufficiently encouraged by the positive tenor of the results that they will use audits as a negotiating tool to reduce premiums with insurers.

Control over Timing. With a self-audit, the firm can select both the elements undertaken in and the timing of the process, spreading it out as desired to minimize disruption and maximize benefits. While outside consultants may be able to accommodate some delay in the process, traditionally they have undertaken audits along the lines of General William Tecumseh Sherman's march through Georgia—continuously and, once commenced, relentlessly.

To some degree, it may be more cost effective (from the consultant's point of view) to do an audit once, from start to finish. This approach, however, can seriously undermine support for the process within a firm and therefore lose some of the goodwill needed for useful implementation of findings later.

Control over Costs. Control over costs is an obvious corollary of controlling the time commitment involved in the audit process. While some firms may feel compelled to "get it over with quickly," many will prefer to carry out the audit more slowly and in stages, thereby spreading any "lost" billable hours over a longer period. Similarly, a firm with the capacity and will to oversee the process internally can save the fees that outside consultants might charge.

Control over Implementation of Corrections. While a firm is obviously free to reject the findings of an outside consultant, there is greater freedom of movement and room for compromise if the process has been internal. If outsiders are involved, particularly if the impetus for the audit came from a firm's insurer, they will likely insist on a role in determining how the audit findings are used.

NOTES

1. Donald C. Langevoort, *Where Were the Lawyers? A Behavioral Inquiry into Lawyers' Responsibility for Clients' Fraud,* 46 Vand. L. Rev. 75 (1993).
2. *Id.* at 95 (quoting Demosthenes, Third Olynthiac, sec. 19).
3. For an early case demonstrating the pitfalls of failing to avoid conflicts of interest between different offices of the same firm, see Westinghouse Elec. Corp. v. Kerr-McGee Corp., 580 F.2d 1311 (7th Cir.) (en banc), *cert. denied,* 439 U.S. 955 (1978).

CHAPTER 5

Successfully Implementing Risk Management

INTERNALLY OR EXTERNALLY DIRECTED REFORMS

Although a risk management audit assessment is a prerequisite for an effective risk management system, it is the beginning and not the end of the process.

Whether a risk assessment demonstrates the absence of tools needed to deal with an identified risk or provides insights into the shortcomings of existing policies and procedures, the critical second step is to turn the information generated into useful, acceptable, and workable risk management solutions.

Here again, the question is whether the firm should do the work itself, purchase software or other solutions developed by third parties, or hire an outside consultant to guide the process. But the considerations, pressures, and benefits of each approach are different from those involved in conducting the audit.

The question of control—over information, cost, and timing—may be even more significant at this stage. Now the issue is less a matter of divulging firm secrets than of deciding on a DIY solution or seeking outside expertise or third-party products to develop solutions for identified problems.

Even when a product is available from a third-party vendor—for instance, a tool to revamp client intake management, or a product to manage knowledge and data such as Intapp's commonly used Wall Builder—some firms prefer the control that developing an in-house solution provides. For others the DIY approach is too impractical, expensive, or time consuming, so acquiring a third-party product or solution is essential. Even then, such firms can benefit from the assistance of third-party consultants to help them make the best use of and gain the greatest benefits from these products. And if no off-the-shelf product provides a satisfactory solution, guidance from experts may be viewed as greatly preferable to a purely internal effort that results in reinventing the wheel.

The role of the firm's general counsel is essential in deciding how to go about developing or enhancing risk management systems. Even when there are other significant stakeholders—such as the firm's information technology department, chief financial officer, or director of human resources—the general counsel should have the ultimate responsibility for assessing the adequacy of the tool or system or policy to be put in place to accomplish the identified risk management objective.

But all the general counsels and stakeholders in the world cannot establish effective risk management systems without the support of the firm's leaders. Developing a culture in which senior management and leadership actively promote and support risk management values is a prerequisite for the success of any risk management project or program, no matter its size. This issue may itself indicate the need for outside help in making appropriate and positive changes in the firm's culture. The challenge is to find the approach that will most easily lead to the adoption of effective risk management solutions endorsed by the firm's leadership.

THE ELEMENTS OF EFFECTIVE IMPLEMENTATION

In the practice of medicine, selecting effective treatment can sometimes be as much art as science. Drugs have side effects, both known and sometimes surprising, and some patients may be allergic to what would otherwise be a standard treatment. So it is with risk management in law firms. Policies designed to reign in lone-wolf partners in one area of a firm may have unanticipated and unpleasant consequences in entirely different practice areas. Procedures established to create uniform systems—perhaps billing or docket control—may prompt a political firestorm from a segment of the firm not previously identified as threatened by such changes.

Our advice is simple. If one potential cure has too many adverse effects, look for another. Precisely because the appropriate responses to audit findings are so closely tied to the particular culture of each firm, this book can only set out common denominators of successful implementation strategies. It will be up to each firm, alone or with outside consultants, to find solutions that conform to these basic parameters. Nevertheless, successful risk management tools have in common most if not all of the following characteristics:

- They are simple.
- They are user-friendly.
- They are, where possible, self-executing.
- They do not add unduly to firm expenses—or, if they do, there are demonstrable countervailing revenue benefits.
- They have the unequivocal support of firm leadership.

Simple Tools

Risk management tools must be as simple as possible. While new procedures may involve changes to the firm's operating manual, complicated and lengthy policy statements should be avoided; they are boring and likely to be ignored. If complexity is unavoidable, for instance when new computer or software is a component of improved client intake management, or docket and calendar control, or new billing systems, the changes should perhaps be introduced in ways that demonstrate the benefits to every stakeholder, including the individual lawyers and support staff who will have to use them. For instance, lawyers are much more likely to accept an extensive intake questionnaire if it leads to more comprehensible conflict reports and faster intake approvals.

Of course, the reasons for and the anticipated benefits of the changes must be explained to potentially affected individuals. Adequate training must also be given to everyone who will need to use the system, and training must be integrated into the orientation of new hires. Furthermore, there are strong lessons from the social sciences about how to introduce new systems in ways most likely to promote success. For instance, selecting individuals or groups most likely to succeed to be the firm's testers and evaluators at the beginning of a rollout process is much more likely to generate positive buzz about the new process or product than just selecting an office or practice group at random.

User-Friendly Systems

Risk management is intended to improve the quality of the services that firms provide to their clients. Risk management procedures that are unnecessarily time consuming or that appear to unduly impede the ability of fee-generating professionals to do their billable work are not likely to be perceived as improvements. If, for example, a firm determines that it needs to improve its monitoring of billing to avoid billing disputes with clients, the new system should, as far as possible, be automated and integrated within the computer system and should generally be monitored in the first instance (unless issues are identified) by support staff rather than by partners.

Some forms of risk management are regarded by lawyers as inherently unfriendly. The most obvious example might be increased information and approval requirements during the client or matter intake process. Even here, however, the principle of user-friendly procedures can apply. To the extent possible, the process should be automated. In addition, and in exchange for the requirement of gathering additional information, the approval process should be streamlined so that the introducing partner can be sure of a response within hours rather than days. Stated differently, risk management procedures can be, and can be perceived to be, constructive. The firm should accentuate the positive and be prepared to take steps to mitigate the negative.

Self-Executing Procedures

As we have already noted, systems that are self-executing or self-enforcing tend to be easier to implement.

If, for example, a firm's client intake procedures need revamping, the new system should operate so that no time can be billed to clients without the issuance of billing codes to assure that the prerequisite checks are made *before* the client is entered into the billing system. And, when potential conflicts are identified, the new system should alert management to the existence of an issue that must be addressed. Ideally, no client or matter number should be available for billing or timekeeping purposes until agreed-upon approvals have been obtained.

Reasonable Costs

If a particular policy or practice appears to be costly, less expensive alternatives ought to be considered and, in fact, adopted unless there is good reason to spend more. We do not recommend being penny-wise and pound-foolish. We do recommend having the right tool for the job. Like everything else, this area will require a reasonable cost-benefit analysis. For instance, a new conflict-identification system that produces concise and understandable analysis—in place of reports going on for pages that consist of raw data—will likely require the hiring of new, skilled analysts, but it should also result in fewer unrecognized conflicts that require expensive unraveling later (or cause claims) and should allow working lawyers to spend more time on billable work and less time trying to figure out whether there are conflicts and, if so, how to resolve them.

Management Commitment

As we have already stressed, the support and commitment of firm management is essential to success. This means, for example, that rules must be enforced and be perceived to be enforced fairly, consistently, and with no one above the law.

TIMING AND IMPLEMENTATION

The timing of any changes should depend on the balance of three sometimes competing considerations: completing the process expediently, minimizing disruption of routine, and obtaining acceptance of the changes from those affected. Significant changes in firm governance or culture should not be unduly rushed, although reasonable minds may differ about what is undue.

In some ways, the same principles that guided a firm to use a fast or a slow track in the audit process will probably be a good guide again at the implementation phase. A firm that chose to undertake the audit in slow and steady phases may well structure its audit process so that, upon completing any given questionnaire, the firm goes through the phase of approval and implementation of needed changes before proceeding to the next risk category. A firm that chose the fast track, on the other hand, is likely to lose momentum if implementation is delayed.

WHAT WILL AN INTEGRATED RISK MANAGEMENT PROGRAM LOOK LIKE?

There is no universal cure for all problems, nor is there a method to prevent all losses. Every firm is at a different stage of evolution toward recognition of and willingness to deal with issues uncovered in a risk management survey. There are, however, some common threads. For example, practice-sensitive standardized forms and procedures will play a major role in risk management, and they should be designed so that their benefits to the firm and its lawyers are clear.

Every firm that undertakes a risk management audit assessment will find that its needs for new or revised policies and procedures differ from those identified by other firms. It is beyond the scope of this book to set out an exhaustive set of model forms, policy statements, and procedures for every situation. To do so would transform this work from a diagnostic tool into an encyclopedia. But help is at hand. Such materials have been assembled in other works, particularly in works published by the Law Practice Division of the American Bar Association. These can be found at www.americanbar.org/groups/law_practice.html.

A TOOL, NOT A PANACEA

An effective risk management program cannot be established overnight, or even over a fortnight. It is a process to be developed in stages. It also cannot be accomplished in a vacuum.

The mere fact that a firm or its management has decided to do an audit (or has been propelled into undertaking one by clients, insurers, or disciplinary authorities) does not signify that the audit will in fact help the firm. Risk management generally, and the audit as the first step in the process, will only be effective if the leadership in the firm supports it from the outset and the rest of the firm becomes convinced that it is worthwhile. Only in this way will risk management be effectively integrated into a firm's culture.

PART 2

Quality/In Control (QUIC) Survey for Law Firms

Questionnaires

1. MANAGEMENT STRUCTURE QUESTIONNAIRE

Partnership/Shareholder Agreement

1. **P** Is there a written partnership/shareholder agreement?
   ☐ Yes   ☐ No   ☐ Do not know

2. **P** If so, how often is it reviewed by the partners/shareholders?
   ☐ Never
   ☐ Once every few years
   ☐ Once a year

3. **P** Has it been reviewed by the partners/shareholders within the past 12 months?
   ☐ Yes   ☐ No   ☐ Do not know

Compensation System

4. **P** Which of the following most accurately describes your firm's partnership/shareholder compensation structure?
   ☐ (a) 100% lockstep (all partner/ shareholder compensation determined by reference to each partner/shareholder's class rank)
   ☐ (b) 100% numeric formula
   ☐ (c) 100% subjective (determined by an individual partner or by committee with no formulaic calculation)
   ☐ (d) part lockstep, part formulaic calculation
   ☐ (e) part lockstep, part subjective calculation
   ☐ (f) part formulaic, part subjective calculation

5. Does the firm regularly circulate comprehensive financial information about the firm's finances and performance to all partners or shareholders?
   ☐ Yes   ☐ No   ☐ Do not know

6. Which of the following best describes the firm's management structure?
   ___ (a) single managing partner/shareholder
   ___ (b) single managing executive who is a lawyer
   ___ (c) single managing executive who is not a lawyer
   ___ (d) managing or executive committee

   ___ (e) a combination of (a)–(e) (explain):
   _____
   _____
   _____

7. **P** For the management structure you selected in question 6, what percentage of time is spent by the individual/each member of the group in his or her/their management role?

8. Are there term limits for law firm managers and leaders?

9. Is there a succession plan in place that encourages the development of management and leadership skills in junior partners/shareholders?

10. If your firm has more than one office, which of the following most accurately describes the management structure of the firm?
    ___ (a) The firm is managed geographically; that is, each office is managed as a profit center.
    ___ (b) The firm is managed by practice group or area regardless of geographic location of individual lawyers in the group.
    ___ (c) The firm is managed using a combination of (a) and (b).

11. Does the firm have
    (a) a full-time executive director or administrator?
        ☐ Yes   ☐ No   ☐ Do not know
    (b) a full-time chief information and/or technology officer?
        ☐ Yes   ☐ No   ☐ Do not know
    (c) a full-time chief financial officer?
        ☐ Yes   ☐ No   ☐ Do not know
    (d) a full-time general counsel?
        ☐ Yes   ☐ No   ☐ Do not know

2. RISK MANAGEMENT OVERSIGHT QUESTIONNAIRE

1. If the firm has designated individual partners/shareholders or lawyers as having any of the following functions or titles, please add a check mark before that item and state the name of each such person:
   - ☐ (a) general counsel
   - ☐ (b) ethics lawyer
   - ☐ (c) loss prevention or risk management lawyer or officer
   - ☐ (d) professional liability insurance coverage lawyer
   - ☐ (e) claims management lawyer
   - ☐ (f) deputy/deputies to any of the above

2. Note: This question should be answered only by the individual(s) designated as having one of the functions identified in question 1. For each person designated as having one of the functions identified in question 1, what percentage of the working year is spent on the work related to that function?
   - ____ % (a) general counsel
   - ____ % (b) ethics lawyer/member of ethics committee
   - ____ % (c) loss prevention or risk management lawyer
   - ____ % (d) professional liability insurance coverage lawyer
   - ____ % (e) claims management lawyer
   - ____ % (f) deputies to any of the above

3. Does the firm have any of the following committees?
   - (a) ethics (or professional responsibility) committee
     - ☐ Yes   ☐ No   ☐ Do not know
   - (b) loss prevention (or risk management) committee
     - ☐ Yes   ☐ No   ☐ Do not know

4. Note: This question should be answered only by the individual(s) who are members of one of the committees identified in question 3. For each lawyer assigned to one of the committees identified in question 3, what percentage of the working year is spent on the committee work?
   - ____ % (a) ethics (professional responsibility) committee

   - ____ % (b) loss prevention (or risk management) committee
   - ____ % (c) claims management committee

5. Does the firm have a written risk management manual, or Intranet site?

6. If so, does it contain (or, even if not, are there) written policies or forms for any of the following:
   - ☐ (a) client and matter intake
   - ☐ (b) form engagement letters
   - ☐ (c) if either (a) or (b) is yes, is there a requirement for independent review of intake decisions, or can individual partners/shareholders make unilateral decisions if they believe there are no ethical conflicts?
   - ☐ (d) time recording and billing arrangements
   - ☐ (e) entrepreneurial activities with clients, directorships in client organizations, and trading in client securities
   - ☐ (f) technology, including Internet and e-mail usage
   - ☐ (g) calendar and docket control
   - ☐ (h) approval of formal opinion and audit letters
   - ☐ (i) evaluation of law firm mergers and lateral hires
   - ☐ (j) identification and handling of professional staff with problems related to drugs, alcohol, or other substances or with problems related to emotional or mental health
   - ☐ (k) management of bar admissions and continuing legal education
   - ☐ (l) response to all actual or potential ethics, sanctions, malpractice, or other claims or problems
   - ☐ (m) supervision of all dealings with professional liability insurers and brokers regarding coverage and claims
   - ☐ (n) preparation, supervision, or review of all disaster recovery policies and procedures

7. If the firm has multiple offices, is there a partner/shareholder in every office of the firm designated to deal with ethics, sanctions, malpractice, or fee questions raised by other partners/shareholders or associates?
❏ Yes   ❏ No   ❏ Do not know

8. If the answer to question 7 is no, explain how such questions are handled:

_____

_____

_____

_____

_____

9. Does the firm have a mentoring system or program for associates?
❏ Yes   ❏ No   ❏ Do not know

10. If the answer to question 9 is yes, how well does it work?
     ❏ (a) well
     ❏ (b) satisfactorily
     ❏ (c) poorly
     ❏ (d) Do not know

11. If there is a manual, is it given to the following newly hired employees?
(a) professional
     ❏ Yes   ❏ No   ❏ Do not know

(b) support staff
     ❏ Yes   ❏ No   ❏ Do not know

12. Is there a formal orientation program that includes training on the contents of the manual for the following newly hired employees?
(a) associates
     ❏ Yes   ❏ No   ❏ Do not know

(b) laterally hired partners/of counsel
     ❏ Yes   ❏ No   ❏ Do not know

(c) support staff
     ❏ Yes   ❏ No   ❏ Do not know

13. If the firm does not have a complete set of written policies and procedures or a manual, is there orientation or other training for the following newly hired employees that reviews firm policies and procedures?
(a) associates
     ❏ Yes   ❏ No   ❏ Do not know

(b) laterally hired partners/of counsel
     ❏ Yes   ❏ No   ❏ Do not know

(c) support staff
     ❏ Yes   ❏ No   ❏ Do not know

14. If there is orientation for (a), (b), or (c) in question 13, check any of the following topics that are covered:
     ❏ (a) client intake policies and procedures
     ❏ (b) conflict-checking systems policies and procedures
     ❏ (c) identity of the risk management lawyer, general counsel, or any equivalent position and his or her role and function
     ❏ (d) confidentiality and the obligation to assist in preserving confidences
     ❏ (e) use of technology including e-mail and Internet
     ❏ (f) calendar and docket-control systems and procedures
     ❏ (g) time recording and entering
     ❏ (h) billing and collections

15. Does the firm have a policy that requires lawyers involved in any proceedings where the firm intends to seek sanctions against another lawyer or law firm, or seeks to report another lawyer or law firm to the disciplinary authority, to notify the firm in advance of any such action?
❏ Yes   ❏ No   ❏ Do not know

If yes, is the policy in writing?
❏ Yes   ❏ No   ❏ Do not know

16. Does the firm have a policy that requires lawyers under a disciplinary investigation or any scrutiny by the disciplinary authorities to notify the firm?
❏ Yes   ❏ No   ❏ Do not know

If yes, is the policy in writing?
❏ Yes   ❏ No   ❏ Do not know

17. Is there a policy requiring that any of the following issues be reported to an identified partner/shareholder or committee immediately after any lawyer becomes aware of such issues? In each case, where the answer is yes, indicate whether the policy is in writing and state the name or title of the partner or committee to whom reports are to be made.

(a) Must allegations of wrongdoing or impropriety made by any person outside the firm and concerning any person inside the firm, whether or not relating to the practice of law or a client matter, be reported?
❏ Yes   ❏ No   ❏ Do not know

If yes, is the policy in writing?
❏ Yes   ❏ No   ❏ Do not know

(Name of partner/shareholder or committee _____)

(b) Must allegations of wrongdoing or impropriety made by any employee or agent of the firm with respect to any other employee, partner/shareholder, or agent of the firm, whether or not relating to the practice of law or a client matter, be reported?
❏ Yes   ❏ No   ❏ Do not know

If yes, is the policy in writing?
❏ Yes   ❏ No   ❏ Do not know

(Name of partner/shareholder or committee _____)

(c) Must motions or applications for sanctions against the firm or any partner/shareholder or employee be reported?
❏ Yes   ❏ No   ❏ Do not know

If yes, is the policy in writing?
❏ Yes   ❏ No   ❏ Do not know

(Name of partner/shareholder or committee _____)

(d) Must the occurrence of any matter or event occasioned by the firm's representation of a client that could cause the client harm be reported?
❏ Yes   ❏ No   ❏ Do not know

If yes, is the policy in writing?
❏ Yes   ❏ No   ❏ Do not know

(Name of partner/shareholder or committee _____)

(e) Must all claims, whether oral or written, alleging that the firm or any partner/shareholder or associate has committed malpractice—regardless of whether a formal claim for damages or restitution has been made—be reported?

❏ Yes   ❏ No   ❏ Do not know

If yes, is the policy in writing?
❏ Yes   ❏ No   ❏ Do not know

(Name of partner/shareholder or committee _____)

(f) Must all claims, whether oral or written, alleging that the firm or any partner or associate has breached a fiduciary duty, regardless of whether a formal claim for damages or restitution has been made, be reported?
❏ Yes   ❏ No   ❏ Do not know

If yes, is the policy in writing?
❏ Yes   ❏ No   ❏ Do not know

(Name of partner/shareholder or committee _____)

(g) Must all threats, whether oral or written, to lodge a complaint with the grievance or disciplinary authorities regarding the firm or any partner/shareholder or associate be reported?
❏ Yes   ❏ No   ❏ Do not know

If yes, is the policy in writing?
❏ Yes   ❏ No   ❏ Do not know

(Name of partner/shareholder or committee _____)

(h) Must any perceived ethical impropriety by any other lawyer within the firm be reported?
❏ Yes   ❏ No   ❏ Do not know

If yes, is the policy in writing?
❏ Yes   ❏ No   ❏ Do not know

(Name of partner/shareholder or committee _____)

(i) Must any billing dispute with clients not amicably resolved within the normal course of the firm's billing policies and procedures be reported?
❏ Yes   ❏ No   ❏ Do not know

If yes, is the policy in writing?
❏ Yes   ❏ No   ❏ Do not know

(Name of partner/shareholder or committee _____)

18. Does the firm have a policy prohibiting any lawyer or staff member, without the express prior approval of a designated person at the firm, from dealing directly with or responding to any question or inquiry from any member or representative of any media organization (e.g., television, newspaper, radio) regarding attorney-client relationships or client matters?
    ❏ Yes ❏ No ❏ Do not know

    If yes, is the policy in writing?
    ❏ Yes ❏ No ❏ Do not know

19. Does the firm have a policy prohibiting any lawyer or staff member, without the express prior approval of a designated person at the firm, from dealing directly with or responding to any question or inquiry from any member or representative of any media organization (e.g., television, newspaper, radio) regarding any matter pertaining to the business or operation of the firm?
    ❏ Yes ❏ No ❏ Do not know

    If yes, is the policy in writing?
    ❏ Yes ❏ No ❏ Do not know

20. Does the firm have a policy addressing alcohol-, drug-, and stress-related problems of lawyers and staff?
    ❏ Yes ❏ No ❏ Do not know

    If yes, is the policy in writing?
    ❏ Yes ❏ No ❏ Do not know

21. Does the firm have a procedure for providing information about resources, including any state or local bar association lawyer assistance program, available to assist personnel with such problems?
    ❏ Yes ❏ No ❏ Do not know

22. Does the firm provide an employee assistance plan as a benefit for lawyers and staff?
    ❏ Yes ❏ No ❏ Do not know

3. NEW CLIENT/MATTER INTAKE QUESTIONNAIRE

New Business Screening and Intake

1. Who is responsible for management and oversight of all aspects of new client/new matter intake?
   - ❑ (a) a single partner/shareholder (e.g., the general counsel)
   - ❑ (b) multiple partners/shareholders (e.g., office managing partners or practice group leaders)
   - ❑ (c) a committee
   - ❑ (d) one or more administrator(s)
   - ❑ (e) other (explain):

   _____
   _____
   _____
   _____

2. If the responsibilities for oversight are divided, is there separate oversight of the following areas?
   - (a) conflicts of interest
     ❑ Yes   ❑ No   ❑ Do not know
   - (b) business suitability and risk factors
     ❑ Yes   ❑ No   ❑ Do not know
   - (c) prospective client's ability to pay appropriate fees
     ❑ Yes   ❑ No   ❑ Do not know

3. Is the form for opening new clients or new matters for existing clients completed on paper or electronically?
   ❑ Yes   ❑ No   ❑ Do not know

4. Is the approval of one or more partners/shareholders (other than the introducing partner/shareholder), committee, or administrator required before accepting every new client?
   ❑ Yes   ❑ No   ❑ Do not know

5. Are all three issues—conflicts of interest, business suitability, and ability to pay—independently reviewed before a new client is accepted?
   ❑ Yes   ❑ No   ❑ Do not know

6. Is the approval of one or more partners/shareholders (other than the introducing partner/shareholder), committee, or administrator required before accepting every new matter?
   ❑ Yes   ❑ No   ❑ Do not know

7. Does the firm have written policies and procedures for screening and evaluating every new client?
   ❑ Yes   ❑ No   ❑ Do not know

8. Does the firm have written policies and procedures for screening and evaluating every new matter, either generally or under specific circumstances?
   ❑ Yes   ❑ No   ❑ Do not know

9. Can the initiating or introducing partner/shareholder authorize the issuance of a new matter number for an existing client without the need for the countersignature of another partner/shareholder or committee?
   ❑ Yes   ❑ No   ❑ Do not know

10. Can the initiating or introducing partner/shareholder authorize the issuance of a new matter number for an existing client before the following areas are independently reviewed?
    - (a) conflicts
      ❑ Yes   ❑ No   ❑ Do not know
    - (b) business suitability
      ❑ Yes   ❑ No   ❑ Do not know
    - (c) client's ability to pay
      ❑ Yes   ❑ No   ❑ Do not know

Conflicts of Interest

11. Does the firm have written policies and procedures for checking conflicts?
    ❑ Yes   ❑ No   ❑ Do not know

12. If the answer to question 11 is yes, do the procedures include checking for the following kinds of conflicts?
    - (a) current client adverse representation
      ❑ Yes   ❑ No   ❑ Do not know
    - (b) former client adverse representation
      ❑ Yes   ❑ No   ❑ Do not know
    - (c) multiple client representation in the same matter
      ❑ Yes   ❑ No   ❑ Do not know
    - (d) business transactions with and/or investments in clients
      ❑ Yes   ❑ No   ❑ Do not know

(e) personal interests conflicting with those of clients
☐ Yes   ☐ No   ☐ Do not know

(f) business conflicts with existing clients
☐ Yes   ☐ No   ☐ Do not know

(g) positional conflicts
☐ Yes   ☐ No   ☐ Do not know

(h) litigating matters where the underlying work was performed by the firm
☐ Yes   ☐ No   ☐ Do not know

13. If the answer to any of the statements in question 12 is yes, how is the check made?
(a) against a computerized database
☐ Yes   ☐ No   ☐ Do not know

(b) by circulating a conflicts-check request to the firm's lawyers
☐ Yes   ☐ No   ☐ Do not know

(c) by analysts employed by the firm to review conflicts of interest
☐ Yes   ☐ No   ☐ Do not know

Outside Activities

14. Does the firm have a policy regarding its lawyers serving as directors and/or officers of client organizations?
☐ Yes   ☐ No   ☐ Do not know

If yes, is the policy in writing?
☐ Yes   ☐ No   ☐ Do not know

15. Does the firm have a policy regarding investments by its lawyers in, or other financial arrangements with, clients?
☐ Yes   ☐ No   ☐ Do not know

If yes, is the policy in writing?
☐ Yes   ☐ No   ☐ Do not know

16. Does the firm have a policy regarding its lawyers serving as trustees or executors for clients?
☐ Yes   ☐ No   ☐ Do not know

If yes, is the policy in writing?
☐ Yes   ☐ No   ☐ Do not know

17. Does the firm have a policy regarding the practice of law by its lawyers outside the firm?
☐ Yes   ☐ No   ☐ Do not know

If yes, is the policy in writing?
☐ Yes   ☐ No   ☐ Do not know

18. Does the firm ever use temporary or contract lawyers, either generally or on specific matters?
☐ Yes   ☐ No   ☐ Do not know

19. If the answer to question 18 is yes, does the firm have policies or procedures regarding conflicts checks before hiring?
☐ Yes   ☐ No   ☐ Do not know

If yes, are the policies in writing?
☐ Yes   ☐ No   ☐ Do not know

20. If the answer to question 18 is yes, does the firm have policies or procedures regarding limiting such lawyers' access to files or information to the specific matters for which they are engaged?
☐ Yes   ☐ No   ☐ Do not know

If yes, are the policies in writing?
☐ Yes   ☐ No   ☐ Do not know

21. If the answer to question 18 is yes, does the firm have policies or procedures regarding disclosing the use of temporary or contract lawyers to clients?
☐ Yes   ☐ No   ☐ Do not know

If yes, are the policies in writing?
☐ Yes   ☐ No   ☐ Do not know

22. Does the required form regarding potential new clients and matters require the following information to be provided?
(a) the client's name
☐ Yes   ☐ No   ☐ Do not know

(b) the client's parent (or higher) entities
☐ Yes   ☐ No   ☐ Do not know

(c) the client's subsidiary entities
☐ Yes   ☐ No   ☐ Do not know

(d) associated or affiliated entities
☐ Yes   ☐ No   ☐ Do not know

(e) names of all officers and directors, principal owners, partners, joint venturers, fiduciaries, and beneficiaries of client
☐ Yes   ☐ No   ☐ Do not know

(f) names of all officers and directors of parent, subsidiary, or related entities
☐ Yes   ☐ No   ☐ Do not know

(g) names of all providers of information
☐ Yes   ☐ No   ☐ Do not know

(h) adverse parties
☐ Yes   ☐ No   ☐ Do not know

(i)   adverse parties' parent, subsidiary, or related companies
☐ Yes   ☐ No   ☐ Do not know

(j)   other nonadverse parties involved in the matter (e.g., co-defendants)
☐ Yes   ☐ No   ☐ Do not know

(k)   the nature of the prospective representation
☐ Yes   ☐ No   ☐ Do not know

23. How much detail regarding the nature and scope of the engagement is required?
☐ (a) scant
☐ (b) summary
☐ (c) extensive

24. Is information about potential new clients and matters communicated throughout the firm to help identify additional potential conflicts?
☐ Yes   ☐ No   ☐ Do not know

If yes, please indicate how often:
☐ (a) daily
☐ (b) weekly
☐ (c) monthly

25. If the answer to question 24 is yes, to whom is the information circulated?
☐ (a) all partners/shareholders
☐ (b) all lawyers
☐ (c) designated partners/shareholders/ lawyers

26. Does the firm have a written policy and procedure for updating conflicts data and for performing fresh conflicts checks when the identity of the parties has changed or new parties have been added?
☐ Yes   ☐ No   ☐ Do not know

27. After reviewing for a conflict, does the firm maintain memoranda, opinions, or notes of decisions made about conflict situations?
☐ Yes   ☐ No   ☐ Do not know

28. Does the firm have a procedure for identifying and resolving possible conflicts that might arise from hiring new lawyers or staff?
☐ Yes   ☐ No   ☐ Do not know

29. Does the firm have any standard form conflict-waiver letters or language?
☐ Yes   ☐ No   ☐ Do not know

30. Is there a person or committee in the firm designated to assist in preparing conflict-waiver letters or language?
☐ Yes   ☐ No   ☐ Do not know

31. If the answer to question 30 is yes, please identify the individual or committee:

_____

32. Is there a policy requiring submission of proposed conflict-waiver letters or language to the individual or committee identified in question 31?
☐ Yes   ☐ No   ☐ Do not know

33. Has the firm ever sought to screen (using an "ethical wall") certain lawyers from files to avoid being disqualified for a potential conflict of interest?
☐ Yes   ☐ No   ☐ Do not know

34. Has the firm developed a policy setting out when and how a screen will be put into effect?
☐ Yes   ☐ No   ☐ Do not know

If yes, is the policy in writing?
☐ Yes   ☐ No   ☐ Do not know

35. Does the firm solicit business by entering beauty contests or responding to requests for proposals?
☐ Yes   ☐ No   ☐ Do not know

36. If the answer to question 35 is yes, does the firm have policies and procedures to review the potential for conflicts before participating?
☐ Yes   ☐ No   ☐ Do not know

37. If the answer to question 36 is yes, do the procedures include the following?
(a)   requiring that a new client form be completed before the firm participates
☐ Yes   ☐ No   ☐ Do not know

(b)   requiring that names of prospective new clients to be solicited by beauty contests be circulated within the firm
☐ Yes   ☐ No   ☐ Do not know

38. Do the procedures for evaluating every new client assess any of the following issues?
(a)   the total amount of fees likely to be incurred
☐ Yes   ☐ No   ☐ Do not know

(b)   the amount of fees likely to be incurred within the first 90 days
☐ Yes   ☐ No   ☐ Do not know

(c) the client's ability to pay the total amount of fees likely to be incurred
☐ Yes ☐ No ☐ Do not know

(d) the client's ability to pay the fees likely to be incurred within the first 90 days
☐ Yes ☐ No ☐ Do not know

(e) whether the amount of the retainer is less than the estimate of fees likely to be incurred in the first 90 days (if less, explain why)
☐ Yes ☐ No ☐ Do not know

(f) the client's likelihood of refusing to pay fees as agreed
☐ Yes ☐ No ☐ Do not know

(g) the firm's ability to meet the client's expectations as to the outcome
☐ Yes ☐ No ☐ Do not know

(h) the substantive and procedural expertise required for the representation and the ability of firm lawyers to competently handle the engagement
☐ Yes ☐ No ☐ Do not know

(i) the prospective client's prior relationships with lawyers and other professionals
☐ Yes ☐ No ☐ Do not know

(j) the prospective client's litigation history
☐ Yes ☐ No ☐ Do not know

(k) potential "issues" conflicts between the prospective client and existing clients
☐ Yes ☐ No ☐ Do not know

(l) the terms of the engagement letter
☐ Yes ☐ No ☐ Do not know

39. Is it possible for a lawyer to open a new matter file for an existing client whose accounts receivable is more than 90 days overdue without obtaining specific approval from someone in management?
☐ Yes ☐ No ☐ Do not know

40. Does the firm's billing system allow time to be recorded on a new matter before any of the following events?
(a) completing all of the client intake procedure requirements
☐ Yes ☐ No ☐ Do not know

(b) obtaining approval to open the file from the partner/shareholder or committee responsible for intake and conflict reviews
☐ Yes ☐ No ☐ Do not know

(c) mailing a proposed engagement letter to the client
☐ Yes ☐ No ☐ Do not know

(d) receiving a countersigned engagement letter from the client
☐ Yes ☐ No ☐ Do not know

41. Does the firm's billing system allow time to be stored in a temporary or similar category and entered later into the billing system when a client number is issued?
☐ Yes ☐ No ☐ Do not know

42. If the answer to question 41 is yes, how long can time be "parked" in this way?
☐ (a) one week
☐ (b) one month
☐ (c) indefinitely
☐ (d) do not know

43. Does the firm permit lawyers to maintain "general" files for any of its clients?
☐ Yes ☐ No ☐ Do not know

44. If the answer to question 43 is yes, is there a policy prohibiting the use of general files for new matters for the same client when any third party is involved?
☐ Yes ☐ No ☐ Do not know

45. If the answer to question 44 is no, is there a policy, form, or procedure for checking conflicts before recording time in a general file or opening a new matter whenever a new third party is involved in the engagement as an adversary or interested party?
☐ Yes ☐ No ☐ Do not know

Assigning Personnel to Clients/Matters

46. Are any matters permitted to be handled by a single lawyer without regular review by a second lawyer?
☐ Yes ☐ No ☐ Do not know

Accepting Representation:
Engagement Letters

47. Does the firm have a policy requiring that engagement letters be used for new clients?
☐ Yes ☐ No ☐ Do not know

48. Specify any clients, matters, or situations excepted from the requirement of using an engagement letter:

_____

_____

49. Are standard form engagement letters available to everyone in the firm?
❐ Yes   ❐ No   ❐ Do not know

50. Are there different form engagement letters for different types of matters or clients?
❐ Yes   ❐ No   ❐ Do not know

51. Other than the introducing lawyer, is there a partner/shareholder or committee responsible for reviewing engagement letters sent to clients to ensure that the letters conform to the standard forms or to approve variations?
❐ Yes   ❐ No   ❐ Do not know

52. If the answer to question 51 is yes, identify any such partner/shareholder or committee:

_____

_____

53. Do individual lawyers have unilateral authority to use engagement letters that differ from the firm's standard form engagement letters?
❐ Yes   ❐ No   ❐ Do not know

54. Is there a policy requiring that engagement letters be countersigned by the client?
❐ Yes   ❐ No   ❐ Do not know

55. If the answer to question 54 is yes, specify any categories of clients or situations excepted from that requirement:

_____

_____

56. If the answer to question 54 is yes, is there a policy requiring that the countersigned letter be returned before work is allowed to commence?
❐ Yes   ❐ No   ❐ Do not know

57. If the answer to question 56 is yes, is there a policy for dealing with the situation where the client has not returned a countersigned engagement letter?
❐ Yes   ❐ No   ❐ Do not know

58. If the answer to question 54 is yes, is compliance with that requirement monitored by the firm?
❐ Yes   ❐ No   ❐ Do not know

59. If the answer to question 58 is yes, are matters automatically closed and nonengagement letters dispatched if no countersigned copy of the engagement letter is received within a designated time or other approval obtained?
❐ Yes   ❐ No   ❐ Do not know

60. Is there a policy requiring that client-provided "guidelines" or policies (e.g., waiver, billing, technology) be reviewed by the general counsel or another individual other than the introducing lawyer before the engagement is accepted?
❐ Yes   ❐ No   ❐ Do not know

Terms of the Engagement

61. Do any new engagements involve nonrefundable retainers or advances?
❐ Yes   ❐ No   ❐ Do not know

62. Do any new engagement billing arrangements penalize the client for exercising its right to discharge the firm for no reason (e.g., by allowing the firm to keep a certain amount of money)?
❐ Yes   ❐ No   ❐ Do not know

63. Has any engagement involved any element of entrepreneurial involvement in the client's business by the firm or any of its individual lawyers as part of the fee arrangement?
❐ Yes   ❐ No   ❐ Do not know

64. Is there a partner/shareholder or committee with the authority to terminate clients if they do not adhere to the terms of the engagement letter?
❐ Yes   ❐ No   ❐ Do not know

65. If the answer to question 64 is yes, please identify the partner/shareholder or committee:

_____

_____

Declining Matters: Nonengagement Letters

66. Does the firm have a policy requiring that a letter be sent to all persons and entities who consult the firm but where either the firm or the prospective client declines the engagement?
❐ Yes   ❐ No   ❐ Do not know

67. Does the firm have standard nonengagement letters that are available to the lawyers in the firm?
❐ Yes   ❐ No   ❐ Do not know

68. If the prospective client has provided information or been interviewed, is that person's name placed in the firm's conflicts-checking system database?
❐ Yes   ❐ No   ❐ Do not know

Referrals

69. Does the firm have a policy regarding whether lawyers may refer actual or prospective clients to lawyers outside the firm?
❐ Yes   ❐ No   ❐ Do not know

70. Does the firm have a policy requiring that, whenever a referral is made, a nonengagement letter be sent?
❐ Yes   ❐ No   ❐ Do not know

4. CLIENT RELATIONS, FEES, BILLING, AND COLLECTIONS QUESTIONNAIRE

Confidentiality

1. Does the firm have a policy for all lawyers and support staff explaining the applicable duties to preserve client confidences?
   ❒ Yes ❒ No ❒ Do not know

2. If the answer to question 1 is yes, does the policy define confidential information as all information acquired by the firm in connection with any client engagement?
   ❒ Yes ❒ No ❒ Do not know

3. If the answer to question 1 is yes, does the policy prohibit leaving confidential papers in open or public areas?
   ❒ Yes ❒ No ❒ Do not know

4. If the answer to question 1 is yes, does the policy prohibit leaving computer monitors on in places where they can be easily seen by passersby?
   ❒ Yes ❒ No ❒ Do not know

5. If the answer to question 1 is yes, does the policy prohibit visitors from walking through the firm's offices unescorted?
   ❒ Yes ❒ No ❒ Do not know

6. If the answer to question 1 is yes, does the policy discuss the use of e-mail, faxes, and mobile or cell phones?
   ❒ Yes ❒ No ❒ Do not know

7. If the answer to question 1 is yes, is the policy part of a lawyers or employees manual?
   ❒ Yes ❒ No ❒ Do not know

8. If the answer to question 1 is yes, is the policy specifically brought to the attention of all new employees (including laterally hired lawyers) as part of any formal orientation process?
   ❒ Yes ❒ No ❒ Do not know

9. If the firm conducts orientation for newly hired professional employees, is the confidentiality policy specifically addressed?
   ❒ Yes ❒ No ❒ Do not know

10. If the firm conducts orientation for newly hired support staff, is the confidentiality policy specifically addressed?
    ❒ Yes ❒ No ❒ Do not know

11. When the firm accepts a new client, does the firm have a policy requiring that clients be advised in the engagement letter of the risks to attorney-client confidentiality associated with the technologies likely to be used?
    ❒ Yes ❒ No ❒ Do not know

12. (a) When the client is an individual, is there a firm policy requiring that the client be notified prior to or at the time of engagement of the dangers of loss of confidentiality and privilege from using employer- or third-party-owned e-mail addresses or hardware and advising against such communications?
    ❒ Yes ❒ No ❒ Do not know

    (b) In any other engagement in which the firm believes a client would suffer harm from disclosure of the client's secret information, please check any of the following issues about which the firm has a policy requiring the responsible lawyer to consult with the client:
    ❒ (i) whether the engagement involves the client in providing secret information (such as information about securities, or other federal or provincial regulatory filings, trade secrets, intellectual property, or proprietary business information)
    ❒ (ii) what means of technology the client wants the firm to use when communicating with the client
    ❒ (iii) the dangers of using, or obtaining the client's consent to the firm's using, the following technologies:
    ❒ a. cell phones
    ❒ b. facsimile (fax)
    ❒ c. unencrypted e-mail
    ❒ d. intranet
    ❒ e. cloud computing
    ❒ f. texting

Client Communications

13. Does the firm have a policy requiring regular or periodic communication with clients?
    ❒ Yes ❒ No ❒ Do not know

14. If the answer to question 13 is yes, does the policy address the following issues?

(a) frequency of communication
☐ Yes   ☐ No   ☐ Do not know

(b) kind of information that needs to be communicated to clients
☐ Yes   ☐ No   ☐ Do not know

(c) which client communications should be in writing
☐ Yes   ☐ No   ☐ Do not know

(d) time requirements regarding returning clients' e-mails and telephone calls
☐ Yes   ☐ No   ☐ Do not know

(e) frequency of status reports for clients
☐ Yes   ☐ No   ☐ Do not know

(f) explanation of the matter's status and progress with every bill
☐ Yes   ☐ No   ☐ Do not know

(g) specific circumstances under which special status reports should be sent to clients
☐ Yes   ☐ No   ☐ Do not know

(h) client copies of significant correspondence, pleadings, etc., both prepared and received by the firm
☐ Yes   ☐ No   ☐ Do not know

15. Has the firm adopted a procedure for seeking client feedback on the quality of client service and the work product of its lawyers?
☐ Yes   ☐ No   ☐ Do not know

Recording Time

16. Does the firm have a policy regarding when time must be recorded and entered in the billing system?
☐ Yes   ☐ No   ☐ Do not know

17. If the answer to question 16 is yes, how often does the policy require the time to be entered?
☐ (a) daily
☐ (b) weekly
☐ (c) monthly
☐ (d) other

18. Does the firm actively monitor compliance with the policies for time recording and entry?
☐ Yes   ☐ No   ☐ Do not know

19. Are there any penalties if time is recorded late:

(a) by associates
☐ Yes   ☐ No   ☐ Do not know

(b) by partners
☐ Yes   ☐ No   ☐ Do not know

20. Regardless of the relevant policies, are you aware of lawyers who wait until the end of each month to enter their time into the billing system?
☐ Yes   ☐ No   ☐ Do not know

21. If the answer to question 20 is yes, estimate whether the number of lawyers who enter their time at the end of the month are:
☐ (a) few
☐ (b) some
☐ (c) many

22. Are there policies and procedures in place to prevent time recorded by one lawyer from being billed to a client as if performed by a different lawyer?
☐ Yes   ☐ No   ☐ Do not know

23. Is it possible for a lawyer, whether a billing partner/shareholder or other, to increase the amount of time recorded on a matter after the time has been entered in the billing system (other than to correct typographical errors or conform two lawyers' entries for the same activity)?
☐ Yes   ☐ No   ☐ Do not know

Billing

24. Is there any policy or procedure to prevent bills from being sent to new clients before there is any record of formal engagement?
☐ Yes   ☐ No   ☐ Do not know

25. Does the firm have a policy or procedure for reviewing bills before they are sent out by anyone other than the billing partner/shareholder, or other partner/shareholder responsible for the client and/or matter?
☐ Yes   ☐ No   ☐ Do not know

If yes, is the policy in writing?
☐ Yes   ☐ No   ☐ Do not know

26. If the answer to question 25 is yes, is the reviewer
☐ (a) a lawyer
☐ (b) an administrator

27. Does the reviewer check the following issues?

    (a) Billing rates are consistent with those in the engagement letter or fee agreement.
    ❐ Yes   ❐ No   ❐ Do not know

    (b) Time recorded is by personnel assigned to work on the matter.
    ❐ Yes   ❐ No   ❐ Do not know

    (c) The work described is appropriate to the engagement.
    ❐ Yes   ❐ No   ❐ Do not know

    (d) The client is not being billed for impossible charges (such as a 27-hour day) or unauthorized charges (such as travel time).
    ❐ Yes   ❐ No   ❐ Do not know

    (e) Time entries have not been increased following their original entry (other than to correct typographical errors or to conform multiple lawyers' entries for the same activity).
    ❐ Yes   ❐ No   ❐ Do not know

    (f) Time has not been moved from one timekeeper to another.
    ❐ Yes   ❐ No   ❐ Do not know

28. If the reviewer finds a problem with a bill, to whom does the reviewer refer the problem?

    _____

    _____

29. If the reviewer finds a problem with a bill, can the billing partner/shareholder unilaterally insist on sending the bill out unchanged without referring the matter to any other partner/shareholder or committee?
    ❐ Yes   ❐ No   ❐ Do not know

30. Have any such problems been discovered in bills during the past year?
    ❐ Yes   ❐ No   ❐ Do not know

31. If so, were they referred to the person or committee designated by the firm to review such matters?
    ❐ Yes   ❐ No   ❐ Do not know

32. Were the problems resolved appropriately?
    ❐ Yes   ❐ No   ❐ Do not know

33. If a client disputes a bill, can the billing partner/shareholder or other partner/shareholder responsible for the client relationship unilaterally resolve the dispute without referring the matter to another person or committee?
    ❐ Yes   ❐ No   ❐ Do not know

34. If the answer to question 33 is yes, can the billing partner/shareholder unilaterally make either of the following decisions without referring them to another person or committee?

    (a) Reduce the bill by any amount deemed appropriate.
    ❐ Yes   ❐ No   ❐ Do not know

    (b) Reduce the bill by a limited amount.
    ❐ Yes   ❐ No   ❐ Do not know

Closing Letters

35. Does the firm have a policy requiring that a letter be sent to each client promptly following the closing of a file and the conclusion of each matter?
    ❐ Yes   ❐ No   ❐ Do not know

    If the answer to question 35 is yes, is the policy in writing?
    ❐ Yes   ❐ No   ❐ Do not know

36. If the answer to question 35 is yes, is there a standard form for the letter?
    ❐ Yes   ❐ No   ❐ Do not know

Collections

37. Does the firm have policies or procedures on collecting accounts receivable?
    ❐ Yes   ❐ No   ❐ Do not know

38. Is responsibility for collections clearly assigned between lawyer and staff?
    ❐ Yes   ❐ No   ❐ Do not know

39. Is training provided to lawyers and staff on prudent collection techniques?
    ❐ Yes   ❐ No   ❐ Do not know

40. Does the firm use a standard form for collection letters?
    ❐ Yes   ❐ No   ❐ Do not know

41. Does the firm permit suing clients for fees?
    ❐ Yes   ❐ No   ❐ Do not know

42. If the answer to question 41 is yes, is the billing partner/shareholder responsible for making that decision?

❏ Yes   ❏ No   ❏ Do not know

If not the billing partner/shareholder, who is the person responsible for making that decision?

_____

_____

43. Is there a checklist or screening procedure that must be followed before fee collection litigation is pursued?

❏ Yes   ❏ No   ❏ Do not know

44. Before a collection action is filed, must the handling of the matter be reviewed by a lawyer who did not work on the matter to determine the likelihood of a responsive claim for legal malpractice?

❏ Yes   ❏ No   ❏ Do not know

5. DOCKET (TICKLER OR CRITICAL DATE REMINDER) AND CALENDAR SYSTEMS QUESTIONNAIRE

1. Does the firm have written policies and procedures for maintaining docket and calendar information?
   ❏ Yes ❏ No ❏ Do not know

2. Is the firm's docket and calendar system centralized for the following?
   (a) for the entire firm
   ❏ Yes ❏ No ❏ Do not know

   (b) for each office
   ❏ Yes ❏ No ❏ Do not know

   (c) for all practice groups
   ❏ Yes ❏ No ❏ Do not know

   (d) for some practice groups
   ❏ Yes ❏ No ❏ Do not know

3. If the answer to question 2(d) is yes, which ones?

   _____

   _____

4. Are all docket control systems computerized?
   ❏ Yes ❏ No ❏ Do not know

5. Is an individual assigned input or oversight responsibility for each docket control system?
   ❏ Yes ❏ No ❏ Do not know

6. Is the system's backup data stored off-site?
   ❏ Yes ❏ No ❏ Do not know

7. Are there any individual lawyers who maintain an individual calendar or docket that is not based on information pushed to them from a firm, office, or practice group system?
   ❏ Yes ❏ No ❏ Do not know

8. If the answer to question 5 is yes, check which of the following persons is designated as primary docket manager:
   ❏ (a) partner/shareholder responsible for the matter
   ❏ (b) associate assigned to work on the matter
   ❏ (c) paralegal
   ❏ (d) secretary
   ❏ (e) docket clerk

9. For any specific matter, check who determines what dates or events are entered into the docket system:
   ❏ (a) partner/shareholder responsible for the matter

   ❏ (b) associate assigned to work on the matter
   ❏ (c) paralegal
   ❏ (d) secretary
   ❏ (e) docket clerk

10. In addition to any centralized calendar or docketing system, do lawyers and their secretaries or paralegals customarily maintain separate calendars for the matters they are working on based on information not pushed to them from a firm calendar or docket?
    ❏ Yes ❏ No ❏ Do not know

11. Can the firm synchronize lawyers' phones or tablets with the central docket?
    ❏ Yes ❏ No ❏ Do not know

12. Does the firm require the use of personal mobile devices that are synchronized with the central docket?
    ❏ Yes ❏ No ❏ Do not know

13. Do all lawyers currently synchronize their mobile devices with the central docket?
    ❏ Yes ❏ No ❏ Do not know

14. Is there a policy requiring that all matters be reviewed at intake for applicable statute(s) of limitation or other entry into the calendaring system?
    ❏ Yes ❏ No ❏ Do not know

15. If the answer to question 14 is yes, who is responsible for reviewing all matters at intake for applicable statute(s) of limitation or other initial entry into the form's computerized calendar?

16. Does the firm's new client/matter information form include specific questions to elicit initial deadlines for actions?
    ❏ Yes ❏ No ❏ Do not know

17. Is it the firm's policy that every completed new client/matter information form be delivered to the designated controllers of the docket control system?
    ❏ Yes ❏ No ❏ Do not know

18. In addition to the centralized docket control system, is there a partner/shareholder responsible for docket control for all files/matters in each practice group or office?
    ❏ Yes ❏ No ❏ Do not know

19. If the firm operates a calendaring system for any practice group or area, which of the following practice areas and activities does the system include?
(a) Litigation
 ❐ statutes of limitation
 ❐ pleading deadlines
 ❐ court dates (filings and appearances)
 ❐ discovery dates
 ❐ opposing party deadlines

(b) Tax, trusts, and estates
 ❐ tax returns
 ❐ litigation deadlines

(c) Real estate
 ❐ contract deadlines
 ❐ loan/documentation deadlines
 ❐ inspection/due diligence deadlines
 ❐ closings
 ❐ lien notifications
 ❐ recording deadlines

(d) Corporate/commercial
 ❐ annual meetings
 ❐ regulatory filing deadlines
 ❐ tax return/financial statement deadlines

(e) Regulatory practices
 ❐ all filing and reporting deadlines

(f) Patent and trademark
 ❐ all deadlines for filing applications, domestic and foreign
 ❐ all dates of annuity or maintenance payments

(g) All practice areas
 ❐ all appointments and meetings
 ❐ all self-imposed deadlines
 ❐ regular communications with clients

Note: If your office or practice group has a computerized docket or calendar system in place, please answer questions 20–22.

20. Does the system provide at least three reminders before the arrival of deadline dates?
❐ Yes ❐ No ❐ Do not know

21. Does the system, and the daily reminder circulation sheets, include all secretaries, paralegals, and support staff?
❐ Yes ❐ No ❐ Do not know

22. Check which of the following information or activities are automatically accessible to everyone operating and using the system:
❐ (a) the completion of scheduled/deadline activities
❐ (b) the adjournment of scheduled activities
❐ (c) the addition of all new scheduled events
❐ (d) the regular notification of clients of the status of matters
❐ (e) circulation of daily docket control reminder sheets
❐ (f) daily docket control reminder sheets that include the timed advance reminders of scheduled activities/deadlines within one week of the date of the reminder sheet
❐ (g) vacation schedules of professional and support staff

23. Are statutes of limitation and other deadline dates recorded conspicuously in the file?
❐ Yes ❐ No ❐ Do not know

24. Is there a lawyer assigned to check the court dockets for all open litigation matters to ensure that all court orders or other filings that trigger new deadlines are properly identified and recorded?
❐ Yes ❐ No ❐ Do not know

25. Are there any lawyers in the firm who do not participate in a practice group or other centralized calendar/docket control system?
❐ Yes ❐ No ❐ Do not know ❐ N/A

26. If the answer to question 25 is yes, what percentage of lawyers in the firm do not participate in such a calendar/docket control system?
____%

27. Are client and matter numbers assigned centrally?
❐ Yes ❐ No ❐ Do not know

28. Does the firm have written policies and procedures for the opening of new files?
❐ Yes ❐ No ❐ Do not know

29. Does the firm have policies and procedures for marking items for filing?
❐ Yes ❐ No ❐ Do not know

30. Does the firm have policies and procedures for the protection and separate
storage of original documents, original
evidence, or other items of intrinsic value
relating to client matters?
❒ Yes   ❒ No   ❒ Do not know

31. Does the firm have a policy requiring the
maintenance of a schedule of original
documents, original evidence, or other
items of intrinsic value in the possession
or custody of the firm?
❒ Yes   ❒ No   ❒ Do not know

32. If the answer to question 31 is yes, how
often is the schedule required to be
updated?

_____

33. If the answer to question 31 is yes, does
the firm's property insurance coverage
encompass loss or destruction of any or
all such items?
❒ Yes   ❒ No   ❒ Do not know

34. Does the firm have a policy for the retention and destruction of documents?
❒ Yes   ❒ No   ❒ Do not know

35. Does the firm have policies and procedures for closing files?
❒ Yes   ❒ No   ❒ Do not know

36. Does the firm have a policy requiring
that a letter be sent to all clients promptly
following the closing of a file and the
conclusion of each matter?
❒ Yes   ❒ No   ❒ Do not know

37. Do any such policies and procedures
require that the closing letter be sent
before the file can be marked closed?
❒ Yes   ❒ No   ❒ Do not know

38. If the answer to question 37 is yes, does
the letter inform the client of the file
destruction policy?
❒ Yes   ❒ No   ❒ Do not know

39. If the answer to question 37 is no, does
the firm have a form closing letter?
❒ Yes   ❒ No   ❒ Do not know

40. If no closing letter is sent to the client or
if the letter does not address the issue of
file destruction, is file destruction communicated to the client another way?
❒ Yes   ❒ No   ❒ Do not know

41. Is a central list maintained for all active
files?
❒ Yes   ❒ No   ❒ Do not know

42. Is a central list maintained for all files in
off-site storage?
❒ Yes   ❒ No   ❒ Do not know

43. Is a central list maintained for all files that
have been destroyed?
❒ Yes   ❒ No   ❒ Do not know

6. PRACTICE AND HUMAN RESOURCE MANAGEMENT QUESTIONNAIRE

New Employee Orientation

1. Does the firm provide orientation for the following employees?
   (a) lawyers hired as first-year associates
   ☐ Yes ☐ No ☐ Do not know

   (b) laterally hired associates
   ☐ Yes ☐ No ☐ Do not know

   (c) laterally hired partners
   ☐ Yes ☐ No ☐ Do not know

2. If the answer to any part of question 1 is yes, what topics are addressed?

   _____
   _____
   _____

3. Does the firm provide orientation for new nonlawyer staff (including paralegals and secretaries)?
   ☐ Yes ☐ No ☐ Do not know

4. If the answer to question 3 is yes, what topics are addressed?

   _____
   _____
   _____

Practice Management

5. Is the firm divided into practice groups?
   ☐ Yes ☐ No ☐ Do not know

6. If the answer to question 5 is yes, are all lawyers assigned to a practice group?
   ☐ Yes ☐ No ☐ Do not know

7. When a new matter is accepted by the firm, how is it initially assigned?
   ☐ (a) to an individual lawyer
   ☐ (b) to a practice group

8. Are there any practice areas for which the firm has only one lawyer with knowledge or experience?
   ☐ Yes ☐ No ☐ Do not know

9. If the answer to question 8 is yes, identify each such practice area:

   _____
   _____

10. Is it possible for significant engagements to be worked on by an individual associate without oversight, management, or review by a partner?
    (a) in your practice group
    ☐ Yes ☐ No ☐ Do not know

    (b) in the firm as a whole
    ☐ Yes ☐ No ☐ Do not know

11. Is it possible for matters to be worked on by an individual partner without the assistance of an associate or review by another partner?
    (a) in your practice group
    ☐ Yes ☐ No ☐ Do not know

    (b) in the firm as a whole
    ☐ Yes ☐ No ☐ Do not know

12. If the answer to any part of questions 10 and 11 is yes, describe the circumstances or the kinds of cases or matters that are handled by individual lawyers without review:

    _____
    _____
    _____

13. If the answer to questions 10(a) or 11(a) is yes, in your opinion, which of the following best describes the proportion of cases in your practice group handled by individual lawyers without review?
    ☐ (a) none
    ☐ (b) few
    ☐ (c) some
    ☐ (d) many
    ☐ (e) most

14. If the answer to questions 10(b) or 11(b) is yes, in your opinion, which of the following best describes the proportion of cases in the law firm as a whole handled by individual lawyers without review?
    ☐ (a) none
    ☐ (b) few
    ☐ (c) some
    ☐ (d) many
    ☐ (e) most

15. Are there any lawyers (including partners/shareholders and those of counsel) who handle most of their matters alone, without oversight or review?
    ☐ Yes ☐ No ☐ Do not know

16. If all work is assigned by practice group rather than by individual lawyer, is there any policy requiring that all open matters be regularly reviewed by the group, a subgroup, or a team?
    ❑ Yes ❑ No ❑ Do not know

17. Is a partner/shareholder assigned to every matter handled by the firm?
    ❑ Yes ❑ No ❑ Do not know

18. Is every associate (or other nonpartner/shareholder) formally assigned to one or more partner(s)/shareholder(s) for supervision?
    ❑ Yes ❑ No ❑ Do not know

19. If the answer to question 18 is yes, are there any matters handled by individual lawyers that are not reviewed on a regular and periodic basis by a second lawyer in the same practice group?
    ❑ Yes ❑ No ❑ Do not know

20. Does the firm have policies and procedures for associates and partners/shareholders to consult with a person designated by the firm regarding disagreements or concerns with the handling of a client or matter by any lawyer in the firm?
    ❑ Yes ❑ No ❑ Do not know

21. Does the firm have policies and procedures to encourage all employees to identify and report suspected alcohol or drug impairment problems involving any employee of the firm?
    ❑ Yes ❑ No ❑ Do not know

22. If the answer to question 21 is yes, is there someone to whom such problems can be reported in confidence?
    ❑ Yes ❑ No ❑ Do not know

23. If the answer to question 21 is yes, are the policies and procedures the same for lawyers and nonlawyers?
    ❑ Yes ❑ No ❑ Do not know

24. If the answer to question 22 is yes, identify that person:

    _____

25. Is there a policy requiring that any of the following issues be reported to an identified partner/shareholder or committee immediately after any lawyer becomes aware of such issues?

(a) allegations of wrongdoing or impropriety made by any person outside the firm concerning any person inside the firm, whether or not relating to the practice of law or a client matter
    ❑ Yes ❑ No ❑ Do not know

(b) allegations of wrongdoing or impropriety made by any employee or agent of the firm about any other employee, partner/shareholder, or agent of the firm, whether or not relating to the practice of law or a client matter
    ❑ Yes ❑ No ❑ Do not know

(c) motions or applications for sanctions against the firm or any partner/shareholder or employee
    ❑ Yes ❑ No ❑ Do not know

(d) the occurrence of any matter or event occasioned by the firm's representation of a client that could cause the client harm
    ❑ Yes ❑ No ❑ Do not know

(e) all claims, whether oral or written, alleging that the firm or any partner/shareholder or associate has committed malpractice, regardless of whether a formal claim for damages or restitution has been made
    ❑ Yes ❑ No ❑ Do not know

(f) all claims, whether oral or written, alleging that the firm or any partner/shareholder or associate has breached a fiduciary duty, regardless of whether a formal claim for damages or restitution has been made
    ❑ Yes ❑ No ❑ Do not know

(g) all threats, whether oral or written, to lodge a complaint with the grievance or disciplinary authorities concerning the firm or any partner/shareholder or associate
    ❑ Yes ❑ No ❑ Do not know

(h) any perceived ethical impropriety by any other lawyer within the firm
    ❑ Yes ❑ No ❑ Do not know

(i) any billing dispute with clients not amicably resolved within the normal course of the firm's billing policies and procedures
    ❑ Yes ❑ No ❑ Do not know

Opinion Letters

Note: For purposes of these questions, an opinion letter is any letter intended or known to be relied on by a third party that is not a client of the firm.

26. Does the firm have policies and procedures prohibiting the issuance of opinion letters (not involving tax issues) unless signed or at least reviewed by two partners/shareholders—one of whom is not assigned to work on the client matter in question—or otherwise approved by a committee established for that purpose?
❒ Yes ❒ No ❒ Do not know

27. Does the firm have policies and procedures prohibiting the issuance of letters responding to requests from auditors unless signed or at least reviewed by two partners/shareholders—one of whom is not assigned to work on the client matter in question—or otherwise approved by a committee established for that purpose?
❒ Yes ❒ No ❒ Do not know

28. Does the firm have policies and procedures prohibiting the issuance of tax opinion letters unless signed or at least reviewed by two partners/shareholders—one of whom is not assigned to work on the client matter in question—or otherwise approved by a committee established for that purpose?
❒ Yes ❒ No ❒ Do not know

29. Does the firm have policies and procedures in place for the oversight and management of any and all reports required to be made to corporate clients or their in-house counsel pursuant to the Sarbanes-Oxley legislation by a committee established for that purpose?
❒ Yes ❒ No ❒ Do not know

Supervision

30. Does the firm have policies and procedures for conducting regular, comprehensive performance reviews of associates?
❒ Yes ❒ No ❒ Do not know

31. Do associate reviews include meetings with one or more partners/shareholders for whom the associate regularly works?
❒ Yes ❒ No ❒ Do not know

32. Do associate reviews include meetings with one or more partners/shareholders or staff persons to whom the associate does not regularly report?
❒ Yes ❒ No ❒ Do not know

33. Do the associate reviews include the following considerations:
(a) the quality of the associate's work
❒ Yes ❒ No ❒ Do not know

(b) the associate's diligence
❒ Yes ❒ No ❒ Do not know

(c) compensation
❒ Yes ❒ No ❒ Do not know

(d) the firm's plans and practice preferences for the associate
❒ Yes ❒ No ❒ Do not know

(e) the associate's goals
❒ Yes ❒ No ❒ Do not know

(f) any discrimination encountered by the associate
❒ Yes ❒ No ❒ Do not know

(g) any harassment encountered by the associate from partners/shareholders or other associates
❒ Yes ❒ No ❒ Do not know

(h) awareness of unreported breaches of the code or rules of professional responsibility by firm partners/shareholders or associates
❒ Yes ❒ No ❒ Do not know

(i) awareness of unreported entrepreneurial relationships with clients or insider trading in securities involving any employee of the firm
❒ Yes ❒ No ❒ Do not know

(j) awareness of alcohol- or drug-related problems involving any employee of the firm
❒ Yes ❒ No ❒ Do not know

34. Is there a policy requiring that partners/shareholders have a regular physical health checkup?
❒ Yes ❒ No ❒ Do not know

35. Does the firm have written procedures for handling lawyer departures from the firm?
❒ Yes ❒ No ❒ Do not know

Due Diligence Regarding Lateral Hires

36. Does the firm have policies and procedures for conducting due diligence examinations of potential lateral hire lawyers?
❏ Yes   ❏ No   ❏ Do not know

37. If the answer to question 36 is yes, is the
due diligence review handled by a single
senior lawyer or administrator for all lateral
hires without exception on a uniform basis?
❏ Yes   ❏ No   ❏ Do not know

38. If the answer to question 36 is yes, do the
policies and procedures for conducting
due diligence examinations of all lawyers
include the following steps:
  (a) verifying academic qualifications
       ❏ Yes   ❏ No   ❏ Do not know

  (b) verifying bar admissions
       ❏ Yes   ❏ No   ❏ Do not know

  (c) verifying bar registration and compli-
       ance with CLE requirements in every
       state where the lawyer is admitted
       ❏ Yes   ❏ No   ❏ Do not know

  (d) verifying claimed certifications and
       awards
       ❏ Yes   ❏ No   ❏ Do not know

  (e) verifying claimed publications
       ❏ Yes   ❏ No   ❏ Do not know

  (f) checking personal references
       ❏ Yes   ❏ No   ❏ Do not know

  (g) checking grievance or disciplinary
       records
       ❏ Yes   ❏ No   ❏ Do not know

  (h) checking for lawsuits and judgments
       ❏ Yes   ❏ No   ❏ Do not know

  (i) checking for criminal history
       ❏ Yes   ❏ No   ❏ Do not know

  (j) verifying the existence and adequacy
       of current and prior professional liabil-
       ity insurance
       ❏ Yes   ❏ No   ❏ Do not know

  (k) checking malpractice claims history
       ❏ Yes   ❏ No   ❏ Do not know

  (l) checking bank and credit references
       ❏ Yes   ❏ No   ❏ Do not know

  (m) checking all clients for conflicts of
       interest
       ❏ Yes   ❏ No   ❏ Do not know

  (n) checking for bankruptcies
       ❏ Yes   ❏ No   ❏ Do not know

  (o) checking for denials of malpractice
       insurance
       ❏ Yes   ❏ No   ❏ Do not know

  (p) assessing risk (and extent) of potential
       claims from prior firm for "unfinished
       business," clawbacks of distributions,
       or claims by the lawyer for unpaid
       income or capital
       ❏ Yes   ❏ No   ❏ Do not know

39. Is there any review by a partner/share-
holder of the firm at the time of the arrival
of a lateral lawyer of each of the files
being transferred to the firm?
❏ Yes   ❏ No   ❏ Do not know

40. If the answer to question 39 is yes, check
which of the following issues that review
includes:
  ❏ (a) docket calendar deadlines
  ❏ (b) parties (for conflicts purposes)
  ❏ (c) appropriate staffing in the firm

41. Does the firm have procedures for
ensuring that the lateral lawyer is
assigned to an appropriate practice
group in all the matters being transferred
to the firm?
❏ Yes   ❏ No   ❏ Do not know

Professional Development

42. Does the firm have policies and procedures regarding continuing legal education (CLE)?
❏ Yes   ❏ No   ❏ Do not know

43. Is there a partner/shareholder or other
staff person responsible for maintaining CLE records for all professional
personnel?
❏ Yes   ❏ No   ❏ Do not know

44. If the answer to question 43 is yes, identify that person (or their title):

_____

45. Does the firm monitor compliance with the
relevant provincial CLE requirements?
❏ Yes   ❏ No   ❏ Do not know

46. Are all professional personnel currently
in compliance with the relevant state CLE
requirements?
❏ Yes   ❏ No   ❏ Do not know

47. Does the firm have its own CLE requirements in states where CLE is not mandatory?
❏ Yes   ❏ No   ❏ Do not know

48. Does the firm conduct internal training or other CLE programs?
❏ Yes   ❏ No   ❏ Do not know

49. If the answer to question 48 is yes, is legal ethics a mandatory part of the firm's program?
❏ Yes   ❏ No   ❏ Do not know

50. Does the firm provide regular (at least annual) training on firm policies and procedures, on risk management, or on handling of potential claims?
❏ Yes   ❏ No   ❏ Do not know

Succession Planning

51. Does the firm have a mandatory retirement age?
❏ Yes   ❏ No   ❏ Do not know

52. Does the firm have policies for the evaluation of lawyer competence whenever a question is raised, or when lawyers continue to practice after a change in status?
❏ Yes   ❏ No   ❏ Do not know

53. Does the firm have policies and procedures for promoting or encouraging lawyers to transfer business and client responsibilities in advance of retirement?
❏ Yes   ❏ No   ❏ Do not know

54. If the answer to question 53 is yes, does the firm's compensation structure encourage lawyers to transfer clients to more junior lawyers?
❏ Yes   ❏ No   ❏ Do not know

7. TRUST ACCOUNTS AND FINANCIAL CONTROLS QUESTIONNAIRE

1. Does the firm maintain an escrow or trust account for client funds, and maintain accurate records relating to the receipt and disbursement of all such funds?
   ☐ Yes ☐ No ☐ Do not know

   If yes, do the firm's escrow or trust accounts in each state where the firm practices comply with that state's rules?
   ☐ Yes ☐ No ☐ Do not know

2. Does the firm maintain safe deposit boxes or similar facilities for client property, and does it keep accurate records of property held in such boxes?
   ☐ Yes ☐ No ☐ Do not know

3. Who in the firm is responsible for the operation and oversight of the escrow or trust accounts and safe deposit boxes?

   _____

4. Are any nonlawyers signatories of any escrow or trust accounts for client funds or safe deposit boxes for client property?
   ☐ Yes ☐ No ☐ Do not know

5. How many signatures are required for checks drawn on escrow or trust accounts for client funds?
   ☐ Yes ☐ No ☐ Do not know

6. Does the firm have internal audit procedures in place to ensure that all firm bank accounts (including the firm's operating accounts) are being used appropriately?
   ☐ Yes ☐ No ☐ Do not know

7. If the answer to question 6 is yes, and the procedures are in writing, please attach them and state the frequency of their distribution to, or how they may be accessed by, lawyers in the firm:

   _____
   _____
   _____

8. If the answer to question 6 is yes, and the procedures are not in writing, describe the procedures, state how they are communicated to the lawyers of the firm, and indicate when they were last communicated to the lawyers:

   _____
   _____
   _____

9. Does the firm have policies or procedures requiring lateral hires to transfer all client funds previously held into an account of the law firm?
   ☐ Yes ☐ No ☐ Do not know

10. If the answer to question 9 is yes, and the policies and procedures are in writing, please attach them and state the frequency of their distribution to, or how they may be accessed by, lawyers in the firm:

    _____
    _____
    _____

11. If the answer to question 9 is yes, and the policies and procedures are not in writing, describe the procedures, state how they are communicated to the lawyers of the firm, and indicate when they were last communicated to the lawyers:

    _____
    _____
    _____
    _____

12. Does the firm check all files transferred in by lateral hires to determine whether the lateral hire is holding client funds?
    ☐ Yes ☐ No ☐ Do not know

13. Does the firm permit attorneys to act as escrow agents for clients?
    ☐ Yes ☐ No ☐ Do not know

14. Does the firm permit attorneys to act as escrow agents for third parties that are not clients of the firm?
    ☐ Yes ☐ No ☐ Do not know

15. Does the firm have a written policy governing when and in what circumstances the firm or its lawyers may act as escrow agents?
    ☐ Yes ☐ No ☐ Do not know

16. Does the firm have a standard form escrow agreement to be used in accordance with the applicable policy?
    ☐ Yes ☐ No ☐ Do not know

17. Does the agreement make clear that no attorney-client relationship is created by accepting escrow funds from third parties that are not already clients, and that the

firm's sole duties in connection with the escrow are as set out in the agreement?
☐ Yes   ☐ No   ☐ Do not know

18. Does the firm maintain either fidelity bonds or other insurance to protect against losses or misappropriations from client, trust, or escrow accounts under the control of the firm or its lawyers?
☐ Yes   ☐ No   ☐ Do not know

19. Does the firm have written policies regarding the circumstances when expenses may be charged to clients or to the firm?
☐ Yes   ☐ No   ☐ Do not know

20. Do the policies relating to expenses require that in order for any expense to be reimbursed it must be accompanied by original receipts and by an explanation of the purpose for which the expense was incurred?
☐ Yes   ☐ No   ☐ Do not know

21. Do the policies relating to expenses require prior approvals from a designated member of the firm's management for expenses over a designated amount that are to be paid or reimbursed by the firm?
☐ Yes   ☐ No   ☐ Do not know

22. Is someone designated as an alternative reviewer when the designated person is absent, or when the request for reimbursement is from the normally designated person?
☐ Yes   ☐ No   ☐ Do not know

23. If the answer to question 18 is yes, are the policies described in questions 19, 20, and 21 monitored and enforced?
☐ Yes   ☐ No   ☐ Do not know

24. Is any review conducted as to the adequacy of the documentation accompanying a request for reimbursement of expenses that are to be charged to a client to ensure that the expense was actually incurred, and was proper and appropriate?
☐ Yes   ☐ No   ☐ Do not know

25. If the answer to question 23 is yes, is there a member of the firm's management designated to be consulted if the reviewer has concerns or if the request or the submission does not comply with the firm's policies?
☐ Yes   ☐ No   ☐ Do not know

26. Have the firm's financial controls for monitoring and managing expense reimbursement been reviewed by the firm's outside auditors within the past three years?
☐ Yes   ☐ No   ☐ Do not know

27. Is there a policy requiring or practice of conducting random reviews of bills sent to clients to insure compliance with the firm's polices with respect to bills?
☐ Yes   ☐ No   ☐ Do not know

28. If a lawyer, member of the support staff, or administrator is aware of a bill that is in any way not compliant with the firm's policies and practices, or its fiduciary duties to a client, is there a policy that designates someone other than the lawyer who generated or approved the bill to conduct a review to confirm the propriety of the bill?
☐ Yes   ☐ No   ☐ Do not know

29. Are the firm's financial statements audited?
☐ Yes   ☐ No   ☐ Do not know

30. Do the firm's accountants periodically review and approve the controls on all firm bank accounts, including client trust accounts?
☐ Yes   ☐ No   ☐ Do not know

31. Is any review conducted to ensure that all firm attorneys are complying with specific client guidelines as to billing and expenses?
☐ Yes   ☐ No   ☐ Do not know

8. TECHNOLOGY AND DATA SECURITY SYSTEMS QUESTIONNAIRE

1. Has the firm designated a partner, share-holder, or senior executive as the firm's technology security officer?
   ❏ Yes   ❏ No   ❏ Do not know

2. Has the firm either on its own account or at the request of a client conducted a review of its technology security policies within the last year?
   ❏ Yes   ❏ No   ❏ Do not know

3. If the answer to question 2 is yes, please identify the type of evaluation, when it last took place, and whether the firm was found to be in compliance:

   _____
   _____
   _____

4. Is the firm in compliance with all client-designated or regulatory requirements for maintaining security of client's and the firm's data?
   ❏ Yes   ❏ No   ❏ Do not know

5. Does the firm have written technology and data security policies?
   ❏ Yes   ❏ No   ❏ Do not know

6. Does the firm conduct mandatory training for all lawyers and support staff relating to the firm's technology and data security at least once each year?
   ❏ Yes   ❏ No   ❏ Do not know

7. When was the most recent training program relating to technology and data security conducted?

   _____
   _____

8. Do the policies identified in question 5 or the training referred to in question 6 (if the answer was yes to either) address the following topics:
   (a) understanding the risks of external threats to data security (hackers)
       ❏ Yes   ❏ No   ❏ Do not know
   (b) use and management of firm-provided hardware of all kinds
       ❏ Yes   ❏ No   ❏ Do not know

   (c) use and management of passwords
       ❏ Yes   ❏ No   ❏ Do not know
   (d) use and management of personally owned devices
       ❏ Yes   ❏ No   ❏ Do not know
   (e) proper e-mail behavior
       ❏ Yes   ❏ No   ❏ Do not know
   (f) the risks relating to standard software tools including "reply all," "autocomplete," and attaching unscrubbed documents
       ❏ Yes   ❏ No   ❏ Do not know
   (g) requirements for complying with the Health Insurance Portability and Accountability Act and other mandated data-security protocols
       ❏ Yes   ❏ No   ❏ Do not know
   (h) procedures to be followed when a data loss or other breach of technology or data security policy has occurred
       ❏ Yes   ❏ No   ❏ Do not know
   (i) policies for the use of social media in connection with client matters
       ❏ Yes   ❏ No   ❏ Do not know
   (j) policies for the use of social media in connection with personal life
       ❏ Yes   ❏ No   ❏ Do not know
   (k) policies regarding the use of cloud storage or transmission of client data (e.g., Dropbox)
       ❏ Yes   ❏ No   ❏ Do not know

9. Does the firm enforce a software update process, including updating patches and antivirus software?
   ❏ Yes   ❏ No   ❏ Do not know

10. Does the firm have a process for managing computer accounts, including timely removal of accounts belonging to computer users who leave the firm?
    ❏ Yes   ❏ No   ❏ Do not know

11. Do the firm's access control procedures address access to critical and sensitive computer systems?
    ❏ Yes   ❏ No   ❏ Do not know

12. Does the firm have physical security controls in place to control access to your computer systems?
❒ Yes   ❒ No   ❒ Do not know

13. Does the firm have a response plan in place for information security incidents?
❒ Yes   ❒ No   ❒ Do not know

14. Does the firm have a program in place to periodically test security controls?
❒ Yes   ❒ No   ❒ Do not know

15. Does the firm outsource any aspect of its computer system or network or use the cloud to store client or firm data (for hosting, backup, and so on)?
❒ Yes   ❒ No   ❒ Do not know

16. Does the firm outsource any aspect of its information security (for intrusion detection, firewall, and so on)?
❒ Yes   ❒ No   ❒ Do not know

17. During the past three years, has the firm suffered any security breaches that caused damage to computer systems or loss of data?
❒ Yes   ❒ No   ❒ Do not know

18. Are duplicates of all critical client and firm records maintained away from the firm's offices?
❒ Yes   ❒ No   ❒ Do not know

19. If the answer to question 18 is yes, are duplicates of the following records and data included?
(a) client and matter intake records
❒ Yes   ❒ No   ❒ Do not know

(b) human resource records
❒ Yes   ❒ No   ❒ Do not know

(c) financial records, including billing and collections
❒ Yes   ❒ No   ❒ Do not know

(d) the firm's calendar/docket and deadline control system
❒ Yes   ❒ No   ❒ Do not know

20. Are original documents archived and scanned for record retention purposes?
❒ Yes   ❒ No   ❒ Do not know

21. If the answer to question 20 is yes, are copies regularly included in the backup process?
❒ Yes   ❒ No   ❒ Do not know

22. Is all of the backup securely encrypted?
❒ Yes   ❒ No   ❒ Do not know

23. Is the backup maintained in servers owned and operated by the firm in locations with the same physical-security protocols as the firm's regular servers?
❒ Yes   ❒ No   ❒ Do not know

24. If the answer to question 23 is no, is the backup in the cloud?
❒ Yes   ❒ No   ❒ Do not know

25. If the answer to question 24 is yes, describe the safeguards taken to ensure the protection and preservation of confidentiality of all the backed-up data:

_____
_____
_____
_____

9. NON-TECHNOLOGY-RELATED DISASTER RECOVERY PLANNING QUESTIONNAIRE

Impact Analysis

1. Has an impact study of catastrophic events been performed?
   ❏ Yes   ❏ No   ❏ Do not know

2. Has the firm identified functions and services it considers critical (i.e., for which continuity is required at all times)?
   ❏ Yes   ❏ No   ❏ Do not know

3. Does the firm have a comprehensive plan to respond to a catastrophic event?
   ❏ Yes   ❏ No   ❏ Do not know

4. If the answer to question 3 is yes, check which of the following items the plan includes:
   ❏ (a) procedures for protecting the safety of firm employees, clients, and guests in the event of a catastrophic event; if so:
      i. Does the plan cover office and building security issues such as violent or threatening visitors?
         ❏ Yes ❏ No ❏ Do not know
      ii. Has the evacuation plan of the building where the office is located been reviewed and tested?
         ❏ Yes ❏ No ❏ Do not know
   ❏ (b) specific disaster scenarios causing different levels of disruption— including contagious disease epidemic, physical disaster, or technology interruption
   ❏ (c) provisions for business continuity
   ❏ (d) provisions for alternative methods for conducting firm business, depending on the degree of disruption
   ❏ (e) procedures for uninterrupted provision of services identified as critical
   ❏ (f) provisions for recovery time frames for all functions and services
   ❏ (g) provisions for maintaining access to computer records
   ❏ (h) provisions for office equipment that can be used by the staff
   ❏ (i) requirement of immediate notification of all partners/shareholders, associates, and support staff of the firm
   ❏ (j) requirement of immediate notification of clients of the firm
   ❏ (k) requirement of immediate notification of vendors and service providers of the firm
   ❏ (l) requirement of immediate notification of mail and courier services of the firm
   ❏ (m) provisions for providing assistance to the firm's lawyers and support staff who suffer personal disruption because of the disaster

Plan Preparation and Maintenance

5. Has the firm identified a disaster recovery team?
   ❏ Yes   ❏ No   ❏ Do not know

6. Has the team been trained?
   ❏ Yes   ❏ No   ❏ Do not know

7. Has one or more persons been given responsibility for maintaining the plan?
   ❏ Yes   ❏ No   ❏ Do not know

8. Was the plan reviewed for updating in the past year?
   ❏ Yes   ❏ No   ❏ Do not know

9. Has the plan been tested in the past year?
   ❏ Yes   ❏ No   ❏ Do not know

10. Has a copy of the plan been distributed to all partners/shareholders?
    ❏ Yes   ❏ No   ❏ Do not know

11. Has a copy of the plan been distributed to all employees in the past year?
    ❏ Yes   ❏ No   ❏ Do not know

12. Have formal arrangements been made for a recovery site in case a major disaster renders the office inaccessible?
    ❏ Yes   ❏ No   ❏ Do not know

13. If the answer to question 12 is yes, is the location clearly identified in every version of the plan?
    ❏ Yes   ❏ No   ❏ Do not know

14. Have critical equipment—and replacement sources—been identified?
    ❏ Yes   ❏ No   ❏ Do not know

15. Has telephone service from the recovery site been secured?
❏ Yes ❏ No ❏ Do not know

16. If the answer to question 15 is yes, is the telephone number different from the firm's normal number?
❏ Yes ❏ No ❏ Do not know

17. If the answer to question 16 is yes, is the number clearly included in every version of the plan?
❏ Yes ❏ No ❏ Do not know

18. Is there an emergency contact list (telephone tree)?
❏ Yes ❏ No ❏ Do not know

19. If the answer to question 18 is yes, does it include e-mail addresses, pager numbers, and cellular phone numbers as well as regular phone numbers?
❏ Yes ❏ No ❏ Do not know

20. Is the emergency contact list distributed to members of the recovery team?
❏ Yes ❏ No ❏ Do not know

21. Is the emergency contact list distributed to all partners/shareholders?
❏ Yes ❏ No ❏ Do not know

22. Is the emergency contact list distributed to all employees?
❏ Yes ❏ No ❏ Do not know

Support Functions

23. Does the plan include administrative and support staffing?
❏ Yes ❏ No ❏ Do not know

24. Are appropriate administrative and support staff included in the recovery team?
❏ Yes ❏ No ❏ Do not know

25. Are recovery team members aware of their individual responsibilities?
❏ Yes ❏ No ❏ Do not know

26. Has an inventory of important firm physical property and hard files and documents been taken?
❏ Yes ❏ No ❏ Do not know

27. Are such documents assembled and organized?
❏ Yes ❏ No ❏ Do not know

28. Are copies stored at the recovery site?
❏ Yes ❏ No ❏ Do not know

29. Are copies stored elsewhere off-site?
❏ Yes ❏ No ❏ Do not know

30. If any systems or records are maintained through a vendor, are provisions for those services included in the plan?
❏ Yes ❏ No ❏ Do not know

Insurance

31. For which of the following kinds of possible losses does the firm have in place insurance coverage?
❏ (a) property loss—firm property
❏ (b) property loss—client property
❏ (c) liability
❏ (d) business interruption (and extra expense)
❏ (e) disability and life
❏ (f) cyber

32. How often is the firm's insurance coverage reviewed?

_____

33. When was the firm's insurance coverage last reviewed?

_____

PART 3

Quality/In Control (QUIC) Survey for Law Firms

Answer and Analysis (Crib) Sheets

Management Structure Questionnaire (Page 59)

FUNCTION

This questionnaire is designed to explore two things:

- the nature and structure of the firm's management system
- the extent to which the firm's management structure and firm culture are conducive to and consistent with maintaining control over the fundamental risk management issues that arise in the course of the firm's practice

To be most useful, this answer and analysis sheet (otherwise known as the crib sheet) should not be read or reviewed until all the questionnaires have been completed by everyone who is participating in the survey process (including the firm's management and nonmanagement groups). Then a three-step review can begin. First, each individual may consider his or her responses in the light of this crib sheet; second, the management and nonmanagement groups can meet separately, and everyone within each group who completed this questionnaire can compare notes; and third, the consensus of the nonmanagement group can be shared with the firm's management. This process is intended to lead to a consensus regarding the current state of the firm's management structure and the nature and extent of its ability and commitment to control risk. Once there is agreement as to what is in place, the question of what gaps exist and what can be done to fill them—consistent with the inevitable tensions between the firm's management culture and the dangers inherent in doing nothing—can be addressed.

When this evaluation process has been completed, the firm can proceed to consider the responses to the other questionnaires. Each of these should be reviewed using the same three-step process previously described. This will yield the same kinds of contrasting insights—what is perceived to be in place by those actually in the trenches compared to what management believes to be happening. Whether there is great congruence or significant disagreement, the responses will demonstrate for each area studied the degree to which the risk management system exists and functions, exists but does not function adequately, or does not exist. Again, based on this analysis, the firm can make practical and meaningful judgments about whether and which changes are required and appropriate, and in what order.

For many firms, the answers yielded by these reviews will be reassuring or will enable them to decide on and implement needed changes to their risk management policies, systems, and procedures. For some, on the other hand, the answers yielded by these reviews may create dilemmas or the potential for internal conflict of a kind that leads these firms to conclude that outside, independent, and specialist guidance is required to arrive at strategies and tactics for implementing needed changes. In that event, help is available from a number of sources. First, many professional liability insurance brokers (and some underwriters) have staff that is knowledgeable and available to give guidance in many areas. Second, the authors of this QUIC Survey system are available to consult and provide assistance and guidance—as, no doubt, are other independent consultants.

SCOPE

This crib sheet, like its companions relating to the other QUIC Survey questionnaires, is designed to raise issues and provoke self-examination within the firm. The central purpose of the questions and the crib sheet is to help determine whether the firm has a comprehensive, appropriately staffed management structure to control the risks that are unavoidable in the increasingly complex activity that is the practice of law. Thus, the answers and analysis contained in the crib sheets are intended to perform two functions:

- explain and define problems and risks that the underlying questionnaire is intended to uncover in the context of a particular firm
- generally review the ethical and legal issues that may arise if the management of these issues is inadequate

The crib sheets are not intended to constitute a hornbook on legal ethics or on law firm management in general. There are many excellent books that cover these subjects in exhaustive detail. The purpose here is to help firms determine whether they have in place systems, policies, and effective procedures to enable them to supervise their practices so that they can anticipate, research (in whatever detail is appropriate), and respond to specific issues when they arise and before they become threatening. The book offers no nostrums or guarantees; rather, it raises questions based on a Socratic model and provides general guidance on the meaning and significance of the questions. This method should enable each firm to arrive at its own comfort level (and, perhaps, the comfort of its professional liability insurers) in the management of its practice.

STRUCTURE

The crib sheet follows the numbering of the questionnaire. For each question—and, where appropriate, for each subordinate part of the question—the crib sheet provides three levels of guidance. First, it reviews the significance of the question—that is, why it is being asked. Second, it discusses the broad implications of each response (yes, no, or do not know). Third, it assesses the level of importance of dealing with the particular gaps firms may have uncovered in policies or procedures.

ANSWER AND ANALYSIS

Partnership/Shareholder Agreement

Questions 1, 2, and 3. The significance of these questions lies in the problems that may lurk in written agreements, especially older agreements that have not been recently reviewed. If a law firm does not have a written agreement among its partners or shareholders, that circumstance should be remedied as soon as possible.

Given the mobility of lawyers today, and the frequency with which firms merge, it is important for firms to review their agreements in the context of the applicable ethical rules regarding restrictions on the right of lawyers to practice law. Most states prohibit, and some states limit, restrictions that may lawfully be placed on lawyers who choose to change firms, based on the principle that the client has an absolute right to select counsel at will. The only universally permitted exception is in the context of bona fide retirement arrangements.

A few states permit limited and reasonable restrictions. Does your firm's agreement comply in this respect with the applicable ethics rules and case law? If there is any doubt, this subject should be reexamined through a careful review of the relevant ethics rules at least in the jurisdiction of the firm's base and, possibly, in each jurisdiction where the firm has offices. In addition, if the agreement contains provisions such that the only way lawyers are prevented from departing it is by in terrorem provisions, you may want to review the way in which the firm operates and the way in which its members are compensated and given appropriate incentives to remain.

Compensation System

Questions 4 and 5. These questions address a fundamental issue for all law firms, namely, the relationship between compensation structure and individual behavior. In particular, to what extent is management empowered or inhibited by the firm's compensation structure to impose and enforce effective risk management policies, systems, and procedures? A growing body of authority supports the proposition that the more a firm's compensation structure is based on an eat-what-you-kill philosophy, the harder it is for management to control the behavior of the firm's lawyers, especially those who generate the bulk of the firm's business. Since large claims against lawyers and firms tend to derive from large and powerful clients, in eat-what-you-kill firms there is a direct relationship between the ability—or inability—to control the activities of the most powerful lawyers through risk management and the ability to prevent or control the occurrence of such claims. Generally, in firms that still use lockstep compensation, there is less incentive for lawyers to deviate from management-imposed procedures to achieve individual goals and greater incentive to be team players. Firms that use various forms of "subjective" compensation systems also have the ability to promote cooperation and compliance with accepted procedures. Firms that have purely formulaic compensation systems are at greatest risk that individuals will seek their own objectives at the expense of the firm by taking greater risks than may be appropriate. However, even firms that compensate using a pure formula may be able to achieve collective discipline if the activities rewarded involve more than simply finding, minding, or "grinding." Accordingly, question 4 seeks an assessment of the firm's basic approach to compensation, and question 5 seeks to determine the involvement of the firm's partners in firm finances.

Compensation systems go to the heart of law firm culture and are therefore extremely difficult to change. Nevertheless, firms that recognize that their compensation systems fail to give adequate recognition to the value of nonbillable activities (including firm management) may wish to consider whether it is appropriate to review and perhaps change their compensation arrangements to foster, encourage, and tangibly support collaborative rather than internally competitive behavior. This includes but is not limited to the adoption and enforcement of enhanced risk management within the firm.

Questions 6 through 11. These questions are fundamental to the analysis of risk management. Each firm must select the governance model appropriate to its needs, provided that the structure embraces three basic elements:

- Both day-to-day and policy management (between full partnership or shareholder meetings) are effectively delegated to a central executive authority in a manner acceptable to and understood by all the partners or shareholders.
- All management functions report to that executive authority.
- Where the authority resides in an individual, there is a clear, understood, and prearranged succession in place at all times, including a deputy during temporary absences.

Effective risk management is impossible unless the firm has in place effective general management.

ANSWER AND ANALYSIS SHEET 2

Risk Management Oversight Questionnaire (Page 61)

FUNCTION

This questionnaire is designed to explore three things:

- whether the firm has designated individual partners/shareholders or lawyers to oversee its existing risk management policies and procedures (and if so, their identities)
- the specific functions and responsibilities that are delegated to those individuals
- the information disseminated and training given to all firm employees regarding their individual and collective duties and obligations when risk management issues are identified or arise

To be most useful, this answer and analysis sheet (otherwise known as the crib sheet) should not be read or reviewed until all the questionnaires have been completed everyone who is participating in the survey process (including the firm's management and nonmanagement groups). Then a three-step review can begin. First, each individual may consider his or her responses in the light of this crib sheet; second, the management and nonmanagement groups can meet separately, and everyone within each group who completed this questionnaire can compare notes; and third, the consensus of the non-management group can be shared with the firm's management. This process is intended to lead to a consensus regarding the current state of the firm's management structure and the nature and extent of its ability and commitment to control risk. Once there is agreement about what is in place, the question of what gaps exist and what can be done to fill them—consistent with the inevitable tensions between the firm's management culture and the dangers inherent in doing nothing—can be addressed.

When this evaluation process has been completed, the firm can proceed to consider the responses to the other questionnaires. Each of these should be reviewed using the same three-step process previously described. This will yield the same kinds of contrasting insights—what is perceived to be in place by those actually in the trenches as compared to what management believes to be happening. Whether there is great congruence or significant disagreement, the responses will demonstrate for each area studied the degree to which the risk management system exists and functions, exists but does not function adequately, or does not exist. Again, based on this analysis, the firm can make practical and meaningful judgments about whether and which changes are required and appropriate, and in what priority.

For many firms, the answers yielded by these reviews will either be reassuring or will enable them to decide on and implement needed changes to their risk management policies, systems, and procedures. For some, on the other hand, the answers yielded by these reviews may create dilemmas or the potential for internal conflict of a kind that leads these firms to conclude that outside, independent, and specialist guidance is required to arrive at strategies and tactics for implementing needed changes. In that event, help is available from a number of sources. First, many professional liability insurance brokers (and some underwriters) have staff that is knowledgeable and available to give guidance in many areas. Second, the authors of this QUIC Survey system are available to consult and provide assistance and guidance—as, no doubt, are other independent consultants.

SCOPE

This crib sheet, like its companions relating to the other QUIC Survey questionnaires, is designed to raise issues and provoke self-examination within the firm. The central purpose of the questions and the crib sheet is to help determine whether the firm has a comprehensive, appropriately staffed management structure to control the risks that are unavoidable in the increasingly complex activity that is the practice of law. Thus, the answers and analysis contained in the crib sheets are intended to perform two functions:

- explain and define problems and risks that the underlying questionnaire is intended to uncover in the context of a particular firm
- generally review the ethical and legal issues that may arise if the management of these issues is inadequate

The crib sheets are not intended to constitute a hornbook on legal ethics or on law firm management in general. There are many excellent books that cover these subjects in exhaustive detail. The purpose here is to help firms determine whether they have in place systems, policies, and effective procedures to enable them to supervise their practices so that they can anticipate, research (in whatever detail is appropriate), and respond to specific issues when they arise and before they become threatening. This book offers no nostrums or guarantees; rather, it raises questions based on a Socratic model and provides general guidance on the meaning and significance of the questions. This method should enable each firm to arrive at its own comfort level (and, perhaps, the comfort of its professional liability insurers) in the management of its practice.

STRUCTURE

The crib sheet follows the numbering of the questionnaire. For each question—and, where appropriate, for each subordinate part of the question—the crib sheet provides three levels of guidance. First, it reviews the significance of the question—that is, why it is being asked. Second, it discusses the broad implications of each response (yes, no, or do not know). Third, it assesses the level of importance of dealing with the particular gaps firms may have uncovered in policies or procedures.

ANSWER AND ANALYSIS

Questions 1 and 3

The significance of these questions is that they help establish the existing level and sophistication of risk management oversight in your firm. This issue goes beyond the allocation of titles to address the allocation of functions. The purpose of these questions is to help identify which functions have already been recognized as important and allocated to individuals or committees to handle. In some firms, to the extent there is any designation, it has been to one individual, while in others the function is assigned to a committee. Depending on the size of the firm (and therefore the scale of the responsibility), either approach may be appropriate. The questionnaire, however, is intended to determine which functions have already been identified and allocated.

Subparts 1(a) and 1(b). The overwhelming majority of large firms, and many midsize firms, have appointed a general counsel. In most of these firms, the general counsel's duties comprise all the functions that would otherwise be performed by lawyers designated to any of the roles identified in subparts 1(b) through 1(f). Similarly, lawyers designated as ethics attorneys may perform some of these same functions. There are now extensive writings discussing the scope of the duties of law firm general counsel.[1] Apart from acting as lawyer to the firm, the primary function is being available to advise on issues involving professional responsibility—or any other perceived problem or potential threat to the firm as identified by anyone in the firm—so that these issues can be appropriately dealt with before they turn into crises. In addition, there is an important educational element to the responsibilities that go with these titles, to ensure that everyone in the firm is fully and adequately informed of the firm's commitment to practice within ethical constraints, and to ensure that everyone is familiar with the firm's risk management policies, systems, and procedures.

Subparts 1(c) through 1(f). Subpart 1(c) defines all the roles normally performed by general counsel except for other aspects of acting as lawyer for the firm. Subparts 1(d) and 1(e) also define what are, in some firms, subsets of the general counsel function, namely, responsibility for obtaining appropriate professional liability insurance coverage or for handling malpractice and other claims against the law firm. The claims management function is sometimes delegated to a litigator even in firms where there is a designated general counsel.

In some firms, rather than designate individuals or delegate functions to individuals, a committee structure is preferred. The subparts of this question seek to determine whether the functions identified in question 1 have instead been delegated to a committee. While the committee structure may be culturally preferable in some firms, it has the drawback of requiring multiple lawyers to spend time on issues that could be more efficiently addressed by a designated individual. Committees also create the risk that response times may be delayed and that individual members may give inconsistent responses.

Questions 2 and 4

These questions are designed to determine whether an appropriate amount of time is being devoted to the designated functions. For instance, in firms with 400 or more lawyers, general counsel will generally spend all her time in fulfilling this role and may well have one or more deputies. Regardless of firm size and whether these functions are divided among designated individuals or committees or a combination of both, it is important to identify whether sufficient time and resources are being devoted to these important tasks.

Questions 5 and 6

As will be demonstrated in greater detail in subsequent questionnaires, each of the functions described in subparts 6(a) through 6(n) represents an important risk management task that needs to be performed within every law firm. Describing these functions in writing and making those descriptions available to the firm's lawyers and staff increases the likelihood that these functions will be adequately performed and monitored. Set out below is a brief explanation of why each item is a matter of concern.

Subpart 6(a). Control over intake of new clients and matters is crucial to the avoidance of claims. A key issue is whether the firm is gathering sufficient information to make fully informed decisions about which clients and matters to accept or reject. Subpart 6(c) asks a related question: are these decisions made independently? These issues are further explored in the New Client/Matter Intake Questionnaire and in the crib sheet for that questionnaire.

Subpart 6(b). The use of engagement letters, the need for nonengagement letters, the adequacy of new client or new matter forms, and issues relating to all other standard intake documents are important to effective risk management. These concerns are further explored in the New Client/Matter Intake Questionnaire and in the crib sheet for that questionnaire.

Subparts 6(d) and 6(e). Billing arrangements and entrepreneurial relationships with clients remain two of the largest sources of dispute between law firms and clients—and therefore of claims against law firms. Again, the detailed reasons for establishing and enforcing appropriate policies and procedures in connection with these activities are addressed in the crib sheets for the New Client/Matter Intake and the Client Relations Questionnaires.

Subpart 6(f). Firms are increasingly put at risk by individual lawyers' use of technology, which can imperil confidential client information. It is incumbent on the firm not only to put policies in place that diminish risk of inadvertent data loss but to actively monitor and enforce those policies. For example, if attorneys use mobile devices to remotely access their work e-mails, are those devices required to be password protected? Does the firm's IT department have the ability to remotely wipe those devices if they are lost? Does the firm have a policy that requires attorneys to immediately report a lost device, and does that policy identify to whom such report is to be made? These and many other issues are explored in the Technology and Data Systems Security Questionnaire and in the crib sheet for that questionnaire.

Subpart 6(g). Missed deadlines place firms at risk for malpractice claims. Having a centralized calendar and controls for the docketing of appearances and submission dates can mitigate against that risk. This question helps determine whether the firm has thought about calendaring and docketing in the context of risk management and what systems the firm has put in place.

Subpart 6(h). Opinion letters of all kinds, including those dealing with tax and securities matters as well as audit response letters, create significant risks for law firms. The existence and enforcement of appropriate policies and procedures before any such letters are issued is a very important aspect of risk management. Again, more detailed information is contained in the crib sheet for the Client Relations Questionnaire.

Subpart 6(i). Both laterally hired lawyers (whether hired individually or in groups) and branch offices are continuing sources of significant claims against law firms, the containment of which requires continuous and uniform enforcement of appropriate risk management policies and procedures. The dangers of inadequate due diligence in lateral partner hire and law firm or practice mergers should be all too apparent, yet many firms fail to do for themselves what they would insist on for their corporate clients. Many law firms are beginning to recognize that the only way to manage the quality of work performed for clients, and the performance of individual lawyers (including partners or shareholders), is through effective practice group management. What ought to be done, and how, is reviewed in the crib sheet for the Practice and Human Resource Management Questionnaire.

Subpart 6(j). Attorneys and staff with substance abuse or mental health issues pose significant risks to firms. It is very important that the firm designate a person or committee to whom members of the firm feel comfortable reporting potential issues when they arise.

Subpart 6(k). It is a risk not just to the individual but to the entire firm when attorneys do not meet their state licensing requirements. Lawyers can be administratively suspended; thereafter they may be engaging in the unauthorized practice of law, and the firm can be disciplined for aiding and abetting the unauthorized practice. For that reason, we recommend maintaining or implementing a system to track whether all attorneys are properly licensed to practice.

Subpart 6(l). This item is self-explanatory. All law firms must have appropriate channels for dealing with ethics, malpractice, or similar issues when they come to light.

Subpart 6(m). This question addresses whether the firm has formally established risk management and insurance oversight functions.

Subpart 6(n). Hurricanes, terrorist attacks, floods that knock out entire city blocks, and fires (or floods following fire fighting)—among other disasters—have caused significant disruption to law firms large and small in recent times. Is your firm prepared? Is your staff prepared, and are your clients prepared? The issues and various plans for dealing with such catastrophes are discussed at length in the crib sheet for the Non-technology-Related Disaster Recovery Planning Questionnaire.

Questions 7 and 8

A frequent problem in multiple-office law firms is that information concerning who in the firm is responsible for risk management may be well understood at the firm's center of operations, but it is much less so in smaller and more distant locations. These questions seek to determine how well the risk management function operates away from the center and whether the identity of the person delegated to handle risk management questions is well known.

Questions 9 through 14

These questions seek to establish how effectively the firm disseminates its risk management policies and procedures, beginning with the moment at which lawyers and staff at all levels are hired and continuing thereafter.

Questions 15 through 17

Effective risk management in a law firm requires that every employee understand his or her obligation to report any problem or issue that may constitute a threat or claim against the firm, its lawyers, or its clients. These questions and their subparts seek to identify the degree to which the firm has expressed these obligations in written policies and whether these policies have been widely disseminated throughout the firm. Only if these policies are known and understood can the firm hope to identify and control problems at an early stage rather than merely reacting to a crisis.

Questions 18 and 19

By definition, lawyers are constantly dealing with clients' problems, some of which may be highly newsworthy. Similarly, the media is often extremely interested in developments within law firms. Unless firms have developed explicit policies to control all dealings with the media, there is a constant danger that client confidences will be inappropriately divulged or that the law firm's own secrets may become public knowledge. These questions are intended to determine whether the firm has appropriate policies in place and whether these policies have been effectively disseminated.

Questions 20 through 22

Alcoholism, drug dependency, or any other form of addictive behavior affects the individual concerned as well as the firm and its clients. It is vital for firms to have in place policies and systems for identifying and dealing with lawyers suffering from any such problem at the earliest possible moment. These questions are intended to determine whether the firm has appropriate policies and systems in place as well as whether the staff at every level has been properly educated.

NOTE

1. Peter J. Winders, *Law Firm General Counsel: Extravagance or Necessity?*, Prof. Law., winter 2005, at 3; Douglas A. Richmond, *Essential Principles for Law Firm General Counsel*, 53 U. Kan. L. Rev. 805 (2005); Elizabeth Chambliss, *The Scope of In-Firm Privilege*, 80 Notre Dame L. Rev. 1721 (2005).

ANSWER AND ANALYSIS SHEET 3

New Client/Matter Intake Questionnaire (Page 65)

FUNCTION

This questionnaire is designed to explore two things:

- the scope of the firm's existing new client/matter intake policies and procedures, and how consistently are they are implemented and adhered to
- whether the existing intake policies and procedures effectively control risks associated with or arising from the client selection process

To be most useful, this answer and analysis sheet (otherwise known as the crib sheet) should not be read or reviewed until all the questionnaires have been completed by everyone who is participating in the survey process (including the firm's management and non-management groups). Then a three-step review can begin. First, each individual may consider his or her responses in the light of this crib sheet; second, the management and nonmanagement groups can meet separately, and everyone within each group who completed this questionnaire can compare notes; and third, the consensus of the nonmanagement group can be shared with the firm's management. This will yield contrasting insights—what is perceived to be in place by those actually in the trenches compared to what management believes to be happening. Whether there is great congruence or significant disagreement, the responses will demonstrate for every element of the client intake process the degree to which the applicable policies are followed and procedures function, or exist but do not function adequately, or do not exist. This process is intended to lead to a consensus on the current state of the firm's client and matter intake management system, policies, and procedures. Based on this analysis, the firm can make practical and meaningful judgments about whether and which changes are required and appropriate, and in what order—consistent with the inevitable tensions between the firm's management culture and the dangers inherent in doing nothing.

For many firms, the answers yielded by these reviews will be reassuring or will enable them to decide on and implement needed changes to their client and matter intake policies, systems, and procedures. For some, on the other hand, the answers yielded by these reviews may create dilemmas or the potential for internal conflict of a kind that leads these firms to conclude that outside, independent, and specialist guidance is required to arrive at strategies and tactics for implementing needed changes. In that event, help is available from a number of sources. First, many professional liability insurance brokers (and some underwriters) have staff that is knowledgeable and available to give guidance in many areas. Second, the authors of this QUIC Survey system are available to consult and provide assistance and guidance—as, no doubt, are other independent consultants.

SCOPE

This crib sheet, like its companions relating to the other QUIC Survey questionnaires, is designed to raise issues and provoke self-examination within the firm. The central purpose of the questions and the crib sheet is to help determine whether the firm has a comprehensive, appropriately supervised system of new client/matter intake control, sufficient to control the risks that are inevitable if new clients/matters are inadequately screened, reviewed, and controlled. Thus, the answers and analysis contained in the crib sheets are intended to perform two functions:

- explain and define the key problems and risks that the underlying questionnaire is intended to uncover in the context of a particular firm
- generally review the ethical and legal issues that may arise if the management of these issues is inadequate

The crib sheets are not intended to constitute a hornbook on the law or ethics of client intake management. There are many excellent books that cover this subject in exhaustive detail. The purpose here is to help firms determine whether they have in place systems, policies, and effective procedures to enable them to supervise the process so that they can anticipate and control the various intake problems and issues when they arise and before they become threatening. The book offers no nostrums or guarantees; rather, it raises questions based on a Socratic model and provides general guidance on the meaning and significance of the questions. This method should enable each firm to arrive at its own comfort level (and, perhaps, the comfort of its professional liability insurers) in the management of its practice.

STRUCTURE

The crib sheet follows the numbering of the questionnaire. For each question—and, where appropriate, for each subordinate part of the question—the crib sheet provides three levels of guidance. First, it reviews the significance of the question—that is, why it is being asked. Second, it discusses the broad implications of each response (yes, no, or do not know). Third, it assesses the level of importance of dealing with the particular gaps firms may have uncovered in policies or procedures.

ANSWER AND ANALYSIS

New Business Screening and Intake

Questions 1, 2, and 5. Whatever information is required to be assembled before any new client may be accepted, the information gathered is of no value unless there is fully independent oversight and control of the intake decisions. This applies to all firms with more than one principal or partner. The key element here is independence. The essential requirement is that the designated partner/shareholder (or committee) have the final authority to determine if, or on what conditions, the engagement should be accepted by the firm—not the partner/ shareholder seeking to introduce the client or matter. The introducing partner should have no veto or right to circumvent this decision-making process under any circumstances—the future financial well-being of the firm and of every individual partner may depend on this. A significant proportion of all major claims against and settlements by law firms of all sizes result from their failure to adequately control the client intake process—whether through inadequate conflict checking, inadequate "smell testing," inadequate fee and billing controls, or inadequate definition of the scope of representation or the identity of the client. If the firm permits clients to be accepted in ways that shortcut appropriate screening and oversight, sooner or later a major claim will arise that could have been avoided.

While some firms continue to have reservations about this kind of independent review, partly on the ground that it intrudes on the prospective client or on the autonomy of each partner or shareholder, such misgivings are ill founded. On the contrary, desirable clients to whom the process is carefully explained should be reassured by the thoroughness of the process—which they will rightly see as being for their own protection as well as for the benefit of the firm and its existing clients.

Question 3. Unless the client intake oversight process can be completed within a short time (preferably in hours, not days), lawyers seeking to introduce new clients are likely to seek—and find—ways to get around the system. Accordingly, firms are well advised to streamline the process of obtaining, circulating, and screening new client forms— without, of course, reducing the amount of information required to be obtained. To that end, while not a requirement, computerizing the gathering and circulation of information enormously speeds the oversight process.

Questions 4, 9, and 10. For all the reasons set out in the prior responses, it will be clear that even independence within a thorough review process will ultimately provide no protection unless the reviewing partner/shareholder (or committee) has the authority to make decisions binding on the introducing lawyer. The issue here is to counterbalance the obvious—and usually commendable—impulse to accept new clients with the necessary level of caution and care to avoid the risks attendant on accepting engagements that carry dangerous levels of risk.

Question 6. While new matters for existing clients may require more limited oversight, they must be subject to an appropriate conflict-checking review. In addition, many firms find it useful to check that clients do not have large outstanding accounts receivable before new matters may be accepted. Accordingly, for the reasons spelled out in the prior responses, some independent oversight even of new matters for existing clients is important.

Questions 7 and 8. It is essential that every firm have a highly detailed new or prospective client questionnaire or form. Accordingly, a "no" or "do not know" answer to any of these questions immediately and automatically triggers loud alarm bells. Without an appropriate form, and policies requiring its completion, no meaningful control of the intake process is possible. In addition, the lack of such a form is likely to lead to billing and collection problems, as more fully discussed in the crib sheet for the Client Relations, Fees, Billing, and Collections Questionnaire.

The standard form for new clients should encompass at least the following matters:

- name and address of the client—and each client if there are to be multiple clients;
- names of all principals, of officers/directors of a corporate entity, or of all persons likely to be involved in the representation in any way;
- names of all related, subsidiary, associated, or parent entities of the client (there are subscription services available to obtain this information for all publicly traded entities);
- names of all entities, and of all individuals involved in the transaction or matter not being represented by your firm, and the nature of their respective involvement, whether adversarial or not, and, where possible, the names of all lawyers representing such parties;
- a detailed description of the nature and scope of the representation sought, including any limitations agreed to with the client regarding the terms of the engagement, and the specific areas of expertise likely to be involved in the representation;
- express confirmation that there are no undisclosed financial interests between or among any lawyer at the law firm, including the introducing lawyer, and the client or any entity or person affiliated with or related to the client;
- the identity of all partners involved in introducing the new client and of all lawyers who will be involved in the engagement;

- where the proposed client has previously been represented by another lawyer or firm, a detailed explanation of the reasons underlying the change; and confirmation that the prospective client has given express, written authority to prior counsel to discuss its representation, including a complete waiver of the attorney-client privilege and its confidences and secrets in the hands of the former lawyer or firm; and an explanation of all matters disclosed by the former counsel in response to enquiry made by the introducing lawyer pursuant to such written authority and waiver.

Conflicts of Interest

Questions 11 through 13. Unless the answer to every element of these questions is yes, the firm is in danger of accepting engagements that may involve conflicts of interest. Many firms also circulate conflict information to all partners or all lawyers simultaneously with the computerized database search. This often helps identify conflicts that might not be otherwise obvious, including business conflicts. This approach should never be used as a substitute for maintaining and searching a computerized database containing complete information about the identity of clients and adverse parties. It is the universal experience of lawyers' professional liability insurers that claims against law firms where there is a credible allegation of a conflict of interest are almost impossible to defend—even if, absent the conflict, the law firm would have an otherwise unassailable defense. Merely checking for adverse, current client conflicts is insufficient. In the authors' experience, the most frequently missed conflicts in the client intake oversight review are multiple client representation and those involving personal interests or business transactions between lawyers and clients.

Outside Activities

Questions 14 through 17. Outside activities of the kinds identified in each of these questions present additional and significant potential conflicts of interest. It is therefore important for firms to identify when any lawyers who are part of the firm engage in any of these activities. Accordingly, if the answer to any of these questions is no or do not know, the firm may be at risk because lawyers may engage in the activities while unaware of the policies.

Questions 18 through 21. Temporary or contract lawyers can create risks, in the form of potentially importing conflicts of interest, if they are not adequately screened before being employed or if they are not properly screened from the firm's client information other than regarding the matters on which they are to work. Accordingly, if the answer to any of these questions is no or do not know, the firm is at risk because, if the policies are not known, they are unlikely to be followed.

Question 22. See the responses to questions 7 and 8.

Question 23. All too frequently, firms permit new clients to be accepted, or new matters to be opened, with only minimal information regarding the nature and scope of the engagement. This situation raises two issues. The first is whether the firm has the knowledge and expertise to handle the matter competently. If the answer is no, the engagement should be declined. But even if the answer is yes, the second issue is whether the expertise is available without disturbing existing commitments and without involving a learning curve that will be expensive and too steep in proportion to the likely billing for that client. If inadequate information is given about the nature of the engagement, those charged with reviewing the client intake process will be unable to make these determinations.

Questions 24 and 25. The point of these questions is that even highly sophisticated conflicts-checking systems have built-in limitations, the most significant of which is that they can compare only the information that is within the searched database. While that database may be extensive, it cannot completely encompass some categories where conflicts may arise, such as former clients and other parties who preceded the inception of the computerized system. In addition, there is the difficulty of checking matter conflicts, in which potential clients, while not directly posing a traditional conflict with existing or former clients, would bring matters whose issues or subject matter raised the specter of obtaining results that would cause harm to or oppose the interests of existing clients. Such conflicts cannot be fully protected against by computerized conflicts checks alone. Furthermore, other types of conflicts, such as issue or positional conflicts, necessitate some level of human review of prospective client information. While there are no entirely right or wrong answers to these questions, firms should consider continuing to circulate appropriate information.

Question 26. Regarding conflicts of interest, one of the biggest problems facing law firms is that parties to matters of all kinds change after the inception of an engagement, but the information regarding the changed or added parties is not always added to the conflicts database. This can result in serious conflicts of interest. Some firms have introduced procedures requiring that the information initially provided be updated within a short time after the initial file opening and at regular intervals thereafter. Accordingly, if the answer to this question is no or do not know, there is cause for concern.

Question 27. Unless firms keep records regarding the resolution of conflict-of-interest issues, they will be at a disadvantage in responding to subsequent assertions of conflicts. Accordingly, if the answer to this question is no or do not know, there is cause for concern.

Question 28. A common and often serious problem for law firms is the conflict of interest involving a newly hired lawyer (or, in some states, even staff member) and his or her former clients or adversaries. Consistent with applicable legal and ethical rules in each state, it is essential to screen for prior conflicts as thoroughly as possible before making hiring decisions. In addition, complete conflicts checks must be performed again with respect to all clients and matters that newly hired lawyers seek to introduce to the firm. Accordingly, if the answer to this question is no or do not know, there is cause for concern.

Questions 29 through 32. One of the central functions of a comprehensive client intake review process is to enable the firm to disclose potential conflicts to the prospective client and existing clients, with a view— wherever possible and appropriate—to obtaining waivers and consents as required. To that end, it is desirable for firms to have form letters ready for use when waivers must be obtained—based on the appropriate level of disclosure required by the applicable ethics rules and the particular circumstances. As with all other aspects of the client intake oversight process, however, such letters ought to be reviewed independently before they are used to ensure that they contain the necessary disclosures so that any consent that is granted will be enforceable. Accordingly, there is cause for concern if the answer to questions 30 or 32 is not yes or if lawyers cannot respond accurately to question 31.

Questions 33 and 34. The use of ethical screens or walls is ineffective in many states absent client consent, except with respect to former government employees. Nevertheless, some courts accept the use of such screens as a means of protecting against the improper release of a client's confidential information to another client. It is clear that even this level of acceptance requires that screens be put in place before the conflict actually arises (generally before the engagement of the new client with a hiring of the lawyer who introduces the conflicting representation). Accordingly, if these devices are used from time to time, it is important that the answer to question 34 be yes. In that event, the firm needs to be rigorous in implementing screens in a timely manner.

Questions 35 through 37. The significance of beauty contests within the general category of client development is that they pose particular dangers in the realm of client conflicts. Since meetings held with potential clients for such purposes often involve the disclosure of confidential information, unless the requisite conflicts checks are done in advance of attending beauty contest meetings, two serious dangers exist. First, the firm may be put into the position of effectively being subject to the limitations of the attorney-client relationship (with its implications for having to refuse subsequent engagements by other parties) without ever having the benefits of the relationship. Second, it is possible that such meetings will create conflicts with existing clients of the firm. It is because of these dangers that answering yes to question 35 in turn requires careful attention to questions 36 and 37. In particular, it is important that the firm have clearly defined policies and review procedures in place to deal with, identify, and avoid the dangers described. Accordingly, if the answer to question 38 is not yes, there is a potentially serious gap in the new client intake system.

Questions 38(a) through 38(f). Failure to require that lawyers seeking to introduce new clients address the basic question of the prospect's ability to pay will often (and probably sooner rather than later) lead to trouble—either within the firm or with the client, and probably both.

Since billing disputes are a frequent source of malpractice claims—and since in any event they involve a great deal of wasted time and effort that could be put to better and more productive use—attention paid prior to the inception of a prospective client arrangement as to the client's ability to pay is an important element of effective client intake oversight. The value of estimating—and informing the client of—the amount of the fees likely to be incurred in the early part of the engagement is twofold. First, the opening stages of any new client engagement always involve significant work; and second, however hard it may be to estimate the fees for the entire matter, it is usually possible to develop an accurate estimate for these initial efforts. In addition, requiring lawyers to make this estimate for new clients forms the basis of assessing the appropriate level of retainers to be sought from those clients. Accordingly, if the answer to any of these questions is not yes, the firm is probably not paying adequate attention to the profitability of new clients before they are accepted.

Question 38(g). Bad clients come in many varieties, but one of the most common is the client with unrealistic expectations of the outcome or total cost. If lawyers are trained to make sufficient enquiry about the client, the proposed engagement, and the anticipated outcome, clients with unrealistic expectations of the outcome are easily identifiable. Similarly, and for the reasons discussed in the prior answer, requiring lawyers to give clients a realistic estimate of the total amount of fees likely to be involved in achieving their desired outcome is a simple way of avoiding unrealistic expectations of the cost of the engagement. Accordingly, if the answer to this question is not yes, the firm is probably not paying adequate attention to the profile or the profitability, or both, of new clients before they are accepted.

Question 38(h). See the answer to question 23. In addition, it is important for firms to obtain this information before giving approval to open a file to make sure that lawyers are not dabbling in engagements that should be handled by those with knowledge and expertise in the relevant practice area.

Questions 38(i) and 38(j). In addition to requiring investigation when clients seek to engage the firm in the middle of existing transactions or lawsuits (see the answer to questions 8 through 11), by judicious use of Internet research, those responsible for client intake oversight (as opposed to the lawyer seeking to introduce the client) can often identify clients with a history of litigating with professionals, with significant outstanding debts or judgments, with a criminal history, and so on. Accordingly, if the answer to either of these questions is not yes, the firm is probably not paying adequate attention to the profile or profitability of new clients before they are accepted.

Question 38(k). Firms have lost important clients by ignoring the problem of issue conflicts. These arise when a firm takes on a matter for a new client that, while not raising traditional conflict-of-interest problems, may lead the firm to take a public position that contradicts the stance that the firm customarily takes for the existing, valued client. To avoid this problem, the person responsible for client intake and oversight should evaluate the nature of the firm's client base and scrutinize new clients to determine whether proposed representations will embarrass the firm by putting it into such contradictory positions. If the answer to this question is yes, the firm has likely recognized and is using this risk-limiting approach. If the answer is not yes, the firm may be ignoring these risks.

Question 38(l). The importance of engagement letters for all new clients cannot be overemphasized. See the answers to questions 53 through 68 below for a detailed discussion.

Question 39. A vital part of client intake management is making sure that new matters have a reasonable prospect of being profitable. If an existing client has extensive accounts receivable, it generally makes little sense to permit lawyers the freedom to introduce new matters, at least not without independent approval. If the answer to this question is yes, this risk is probably not being managed adequately by the firm.

Questions 40 through 42. Many firms have policies and procedures that appear to require that appropriate information be obtained and independent approval received before the commencement of new engagements. But if a lawyer can commence work and record time before the approval is obtained, the entire client intake oversight process is being subverted. Accordingly, firms need policies and procedures that prohibit the commencement of work before the client intake oversight and approval requirements are met. If the answer to any part of questions 40, 41, or 42(b), (c), or (d) is yes, then the firm's client intake system, however superficially thorough, can be bypassed by savvy lawyers. If this is the case, the firm will find that it frequently has clients—by virtue of having commenced work—that it might prefer to have rejected had its lawyers followed the appropriate policies and procedures.

Questions 43 through 45. The use of "general" files creates significant risk that hidden conflicts of interest, and particularly current adverse representations, may be undertaken before the firm is able to identify the problem. This can cause the firm to lose both an existing client engagement as well as a new one. Where possible, general files should be avoided; to the extent they are permitted, activity on these files should be closely monitored. Accordingly, if the answer to question 43 is yes and the answer to questions 44 or 45 is not yes, there is cause for concern.

Assigning Personnel to Clients/Matters

Question 46. The risks involved in permitting any matter to be handled by one lawyer alone (however senior) are discussed more fully in the crib sheet for the Practice and Human Resource Management Questionnaire in the context of practice group management. If the answer to question 46 is yes, close attention should be paid to that material.

Accepting Representation: Engagement Letters

Question 47. It will be apparent from the other answers in this crib sheet that engagement letters—already required under some states' versions of the ethics rules—are an important element of effective risk management at the intake stage. They provide a necessary foundation to the conduct and management by the firm of the entire client relationship. Much more than "money" issues need to be incorporated in the engagement letter. A clear identification of who is, and is not, the client, and a clear description of the scope of the engagement, including any agreed-upon limitations on the functions that the firm is to perform, are important ingredients. The identity of the lawyer responsible for the client's matters and of others who will work on the engagement, obligations of communication—in both directions—between firm and client, collection, withdrawal, and dispute resolution are also matters that should be included. It has been suggested that for long-standing clients such letters should be avoided, since these clients might be offended. This is generally a mistake. Clients almost invariably respect firms for demonstrating businesslike management of their affairs, and there is no law preventing longtime clients from suing their lawyers for malpractice. All clients should have engagement letters so that both sides will be protected by the reduction to writing of the nature and scope of the relationship. Accordingly, if the answer to either part of this question is not yes, there is cause for concern.

Question 48. It will be apparent from prior answers that exceptions to the requirements of engagement letters should be rare, and they should require express approval of a firm's senior management. Any responses to this question should be closely scrutinized.

Questions 49 through 53. Most firms have standard form engagement letters readily accessible to all lawyers in the firm. Often, each practice group will have its own variations. Lawyers should be required to use standard forms or to obtain express approval from whoever oversees the client intake system for variations from the standard form. Accordingly, any answer other than yes to questions 49, 50, and 51 should be a source of considerable concern, as should be the failure to identify the appropriate authority in question 52. Similarly, while it is preferable that individual lawyers not have the authority to make unilateral changes to standard form letters, if they do have such authority, it is highly desirable that all nonstandard forms be independently reviewed and approved.

Questions 54 and 55. If a client declines to countersign a proffered engagement letter, it is likely that the client will, sooner or later, find a reason to decline to sign a check in payment of the firm's fees. Accordingly, if the answer to question 54 is not yes, there is cause for concern. Some exceptions, however, may be appropriate, for instance in the case of large institutional clients that have their own policies and procedures for engagement of outside counsel. Answers to question 55 should be closely scrutinized to ensure that only appropriate and approved exceptions to the general rule are identified.

Questions 56 through 59. While it is obviously preferable to prohibit the commencement of billable work until a countersigned engagement letter has been received from every client, many firms find this approach impractical. Most firms, however, make the mailing of the engagement letter to the client a minimum prerequisite. This can be enforced by preventing file or billing numbers from being issued or time being recorded (or later transferred) absent specific approval from firm management at any time prior to mailing the engagement letter to the client following completion of the rest of the client intake approval process. In firms adopting this approach, it is still possible to enforce the rule requiring client countersignature by deactivating the file or billing number if the countersigned letter is not returned within a fixed time. These controls, properly overseen and enforced, also serve to ensure that all the other intake policies and procedures are followed. Accordingly, the answers to questions 56 through 59 should be yes.

Question 60. Corporations are increasingly requiring their outside counsel to sign terms of engagement, often referred to as "outside counsel guidelines." These guidelines often deviate substantially from firms' typical practices and can be more specific and onerous. It is imperative that firms institute a policy requiring the introducing lawyer to notify a designated person if he or she receives outside counsel guidelines, and that a person or committee be tasked with reviewing the guidelines and ensuring that everyone assigned to the matter complies with them. The absence of such a policy runs the risk that the introducing lawyer may obligate the firm without firm management's knowledge or consent, and may not communicate adequately with others on the matter about following the guidelines.

Terms of the Engagement

Questions 61 through 63. In at least some states, nonrefundable retainers are either unethical or unlawful or both, unless the engagement is only for availability and not for the actual provision of legal services. Since legal fees are generally permitted to be earned only for services rendered, an affirmative answer to questions 61 or 62 should be cause for concern. Similarly, since fee arrangements involving an entrepreneurial element necessarily create a conflict of interest, they should be permitted only after a careful independent review by the firm determines both that the arrangement is appropriate and that the necessary disclosure has been made and consent received. Again, therefore, if the answer to question 63 is yes, a review of the firm's intake policies in this regard is likely needed.

Questions 64 and 65. Just as important as independent review and oversight of client selection is the firm's ability to withdraw from an engagement, to the extent permitted by the applicable ethics rules, if a client materially violates the terms of the engagement letter. To that end, there needs to be a partner/shareholder or committee with the explicit authority to require such withdrawal even over the objection of the introducing or responsible lawyer. Accordingly, if the answer to question 64 is not yes or the relevant authority in question 65 cannot be identified, there is cause for concern.

Declining Matters: Nonengagement Letters

Questions 66 through 68. Whenever a lawyer meets with a prospective client to discuss potential engagement, two things may happen: first, some secrets or confidences may pass, thereby creating a sufficient relationship that the obligations of confidentiality and privilege arise, which may in turn create potential conflicts with other clients or potential clients; and second, some (albeit very general) advice or opinion may flow from the lawyer to the potential client. Even if no full-fledged attorney-client relationship is established at such a meeting, fiduciary duties may be created and lawyers may be subject to disqualification or even damage claims based on such meetings. One good way to minimize the risk of such liability is to follow up all such meetings that do not result in formal engagement with nonengagement letters, which clarify (if true) that no attorney-client relationship was created, no advice was given, and no confidential information was obtained. Accordingly, if the answer to questions 66 and 67 is not yes, the firm's policies and procedures in this regard should be reviewed. Since it sometimes happens that parties adverse to the initial prospective client subsequently consult the lawyer or firm, it is important to have a record of the initial consultation for conflicts-checking purposes. Accordingly, if the answer to question 68 is not yes, there again should be a review of the firm's procedures for meetings with prospective clients that do not result in engagements.

Referrals

Questions 69 and 70. Often when a lawyer indicates to a prospective client of the lawyer or firm that the lawyer is declining the proffered engagement, the client will request a referral to another lawyer. As indicated in the answer to the preceding series of questions, nonengagement letters should not include legal advice. Firms that recommend lawyers to clients that they decline to represent are at risk of negligent referral liability. If a firm allows such recommendations, it should be sure to allow them only to counsel known to be competent and should generally recommend more than one alternative while encouraging the nonclient to make a choice.

Client Relations, Fees, Billing, and Collections Questionnaire (Page 71)

FUNCTION

This questionnaire is designed to explore two things:

- the scope of the firm's existing policies and procedures and controls in the areas of protecting client confidences, billing, and collections
- the extent to which the existing intake policies and procedures effectively control risks associated with the inadvertent disclosure of client secrets and with the billing and collection process

To be most useful, this answer and analysis sheet (otherwise known as the crib sheet) should not be read or reviewed until all the questionnaires have been completed by all those who are participating in the survey process (including the firm's management and nonmanagement group). Then a three-step review can begin. First, each individual may consider his or her responses in the light of this crib sheet; second, the management and nonmanagement groups can meet separately, and everyone within each group who completed this questionnaire can compare notes; and third, the consensus of the nonmanagement group can be shared with the firm's management. This will yield contrasting insights—what is perceived to be in place by those actually in the trenches compared to what management believes to be happening. Whether there is great congruence or significant disagreement, the responses will demonstrate, for every element of client relationships after the completion of the intake process, the degree to which the applicable policies are followed and procedures function, or exist but do not function adequately, or do not exist. This process is intended to lead to a consensus on the current state of the firm's policies, procedures, and controls in the areas of the protection of client confidences and the firm's billing and collection system. Based on this analysis, the firm can make practical and meaningful judgments about whether and which changes are required and appropriate, and in what priority—consistently with the inevitable tensions between the firm's management culture and the dangers inherent in doing nothing.

For many firms, the answers yielded by these reviews will be reassuring or will enable them to decide on and implement needed changes to their policies, systems, and procedures. For some, on the other hand, the answers yielded by these reviews may create dilemmas or the potential for internal conflict of a kind that leads these firms to conclude that outside, independent, and specialist guidance is required to arrive at strategies and tactics for implementing needed changes. In that event, help is available from a number of sources. First, many professional liability insurance brokers (and some underwriters) have staff that is knowledgeable and available to give guidance in many areas. Second, the authors of this QUIC Survey system are available to consult and provide assistance and guidance, as, no doubt, are other independent consultants.

SCOPE

This crib sheet, like its companions relating to the other QUIC Survey questionnaires, is designed to raise issues and provoke self-examination within the firm. The central purpose of the questions and this crib sheet is to help determine whether the firm has a comprehensive system for preserving client confidences and appropriate policies and procedures to ensure that the billing and collections processes are operating effectively but within the relevant ethical constraints. Thus, the answers and analysis contained in the crib sheets are intended to perform two functions:

- explain and define the key problems and risks that the underlying questionnaire is intended to uncover in the context of a particular firm
- generally review the ethical and legal issues that may arise if the management of these issues is inadequate

The crib sheets are not intended to constitute a hornbook on the law or ethics of the preservation of client confidences or of the billing and collection process. There are many excellent books that cover these subjects in exhaustive detail. The purpose here is to help firms determine whether they have in place systems, policies, and effective procedures to enable them to supervise these elements of law firm structure so that they can anticipate and control the various potential problems and issues when they arise and before they become threatening. The book offers no nostrums or guarantees; rather, it raises questions based on a Socratic model and provides general guidance on the meaning and significance of the questions. This method should enable each firm to arrive at its own comfort level (and, perhaps, the comfort of its professional liability insurers) in the management of its practice.

STRUCTURE

The crib sheet follows precisely the numbering of the questionnaire. For each question and, where appropriate, for each subordinate part of the question, the crib sheet provides three levels of guidance. First, it reviews the significance of the question—that is, why it is being asked. Second, it discusses the broad implications of each response (yes, no, or do not know). Third, it assesses the level of importance of dealing with the particular gaps firms may have uncovered in policies or procedures.

ANSWER AND ANALYSIS

Confidentiality

Questions 1 through 7. The duty to protect client confidences is one of the foundations of the attorney-client relationship. In the modern world, where three clicks of a mouse ("attach"—"reply all"—"send") can cause the disclosure of a client's most closely guarded secrets, the establishment and expression of policies and procedures to ensure the protection—as far as possible—of client secrets is essential. Furthermore, while lawyers may take this obligation for granted, many of us can recount stories of a client's secrets being publicly discussed in every variety of public place—from restaurants to restrooms. In addition, support staff, who are not themselves subject to professional discipline, must be educated and bound contractually to comply with the same protections. Accordingly, unless the answer to all these questions is yes, the firm should review and revise, or at least actively disseminate, its handbook containing the appropriate policies.

Questions 8 through 10. Written policies and procedures, whether set out in printed manuals or available electronically on a firm's intranet, do not constitute effective risk management unless their existence—and contents—are regularly disseminated, beginning with the moment at which lawyers as well as support staff join the firm. Accordingly, unless the answer to all these questions is yes, the firm should review and, as necessary, supplement its orientation program for all new hires, from laterally hired senior lawyers to the newest messenger.

Questions 11 and 12. One way that lawyers can establish a positive relationship with new clients is to address the protection of the client's secrets at the time of initial engagement. While there is no ethical requirement for a policy such as the one described in questions 11 and 12, that policy suggests an approach to the engagement process that will reassure new clients that the newly hired lawyer is concerned about protecting their interests and will assist the firm in establishing procedures for each client that will best permit open communication while preserving the client's confidences.

Client Communications

Questions 13 through 15. The most frequent complaint that disciplinary counsel hear regarding lawyers is that the lawyer never returns phone calls. Lawyers and firms that establish policies and procedures for regular client communication significantly reduce the likelihood of client disputes and claims. Merely mailing a monthly bill, however, does not count as effective client communication. For communication with clients to become a regular and routine part of every lawyer's task list, it is vital for the firm to develop both a culture and an expressed policy on the subject. Furthermore, firms can demonstrate on an ongoing basis that they care about the level of service being provided, and that they wish to satisfy each client's particular needs, by regularly using client surveys. Accordingly, unless the answer to all these questions and their components is yes, the firm has work to do if it wishes to improve its practices—and its relationship with its clients.

Recording Time

Questions 16 through 21. There are two reasons that firms need to manage the time recording and entry system as closely and firmly as possible. First, many studies show that the late entry of time involves considerable loss; some commentators suggest upward of 10 percent of the value of time may be lost if time entry into the recording system is delayed by 30 days. Second, since the ethical underpinning of hourly billing is that time entry be accurate, the greater the delay between the performance of the work and the entry of the time, the more suspect each entry becomes. Since fee disputes are inevitably a source of serious friction between lawyers and clients, even when no allegation of outright fraud is made, anything firms can do to manage the time entry and recording process constitutes important—and valuable—risk management. If the answer to questions 16 or 18 is not yes, the firm likely has significant work to do in this area. The only fully acceptable answer to question 17 is "daily" or almost so. What is important in considering answers to question 18 is whether the firm is effectively enforcing prompt time entry and recording by all its lawyers. In connection with question 19, firm culture will determine whether penalties, inducements, or other techniques will best accomplish uniform compliance with strict time entry and recording policies. And the answers to questions 20 and 21 should give a clear indication of the degree of success the firm is achieving in this regard.

Questions 22 and 23. From time to time there is widespread media coverage of allegations of billing fraud by a law firm senior partner. The allegations may include bill padding and the movement of time entries among lawyers on a massive scale and over an extended period. The only way to be certain that such activities cannot occur in a firm is to have fully articulated policies for time entry and recording that delineate circumstances in which changes may and may not be made during the billing process, and to police the time entry and billing processes. Accordingly, unless the answer to question 22 is uniformly yes and to question 23 uniformly no, the firm should review both the policies and procedures in place regarding time entry and billing.

Billing

Questions 24 through 28. Fee disputes with clients constitute serious risks on a number of levels. First, professional liability insurers uniformly indicate that a high proportion of claims begin as fee disputes. Second, by definition, whenever a lawyer or firm is involved in a fee dispute, the time spent dealing with this issue is time that might otherwise have been spent productively. Third, when billing disputes become public, and especially when they involve allegations of billing improprieties, the firm's reputation is at stake. Accordingly, the failure to have in place clearly expressed, comprehensive policies covering every aspect of the billing process constitutes a real risk to the firm. These policies should encompass at least the issues raised in this series of questions. Self-evidently, the time recording and billing system should not permit, under any circumstance, the issuance of a bill before the completion of the client intake approval process. While the review of bills was traditionally left to each billing or other responsible partner, the failure to have independent review—at least at the administrative level within the back-office department that prepares bills—can lead, all too easily, to the situation where the firm first learns of allegations of billing impropriety in the press. When bills are reviewed, all the issues listed in the subparts of question 27 should be addressed. And if a question or issue arises, the reviewer should have a specific direction as to which firm leader should be consulted (most appropriately, the firm's general counsel or ethics partner). Accordingly, the answer to all these questions needs to be yes (except question 26, for which an affirmative answer to either part is equally appropriate) if the firm is to be sure of reducing fee disputes based on the contents of its bills and of minimizing the fallout from any disputes that do occur.

Question 29. Unless the person with the ultimate authority over the billing process has authority to prevent bills from being issued over the objection of the billing or responsible partner, the review system is inadequate. Accordingly, if the firm is to be effectively shielded from the risks described in the previous answer, it is essential that the answer to this question be uniformly no.

Questions 30 through 32. The answers given to these questions by those completing this questionnaire will give a very clear indication to the firm's management whether the current policies and procedures are effective in shielding the firm from the risks described in the previous answers.

Questions 33 and 34. While it is customary to permit billing or other responsible partners to reduce bills by a limited amount, even this practice should be carefully circumscribed. The authors are aware of cases where time charges were moved among different lawyers so that, even though bills were lower than they would have been if the time were allocated to the lawyers who actually performed the work, billing fraud was nevertheless alleged. Although it may be too burdensome to eliminate transfers, they should be permitted only within the context of the kind of clear overall policies described in the previous answers. Furthermore, the discretion to settle or reduce bills should be very clearly limited, with the resolution of all significant disputes and reductions being independently reviewed and approved. Accordingly, the answers to these questions should be carefully considered to determine whether the appropriate policies are in place and understood.

Closing Letters

Questions 35 and 36. There are three reasons that law firms need a policy requiring the prompt sending of closing letters after the closing of a file and conclusion of each matter, as well as procedures to enforce that policy. The first reason relates directly to client intake. The rules governing conflicts of interest treat current and former clients differently. Absent consent of all concerned, engagements adverse to current clients are always prohibited. On the other hand, lawyers may be adverse to former clients unless the new engagement is the same or substantially related to the prior engagement, or the lawyer in question learned secrets or confidences during the prior engagement that are related to the proposed new engagement. Accordingly, by sending closing letters, lawyers and their firms expand the universe of former clients, and thereby expand the universe of matters they may accept in the future. The second reason for using closing letters is to avoid liability for acts and omissions in the future by clearly indicating to the client that the lawyer or firm has ceased to provide services to the client. In a number of cases, firms did not advise clients of changes in the law or take steps to protect a client's interest because they believed that their representation had long since ceased; the client, however, believed the lawyer or firm continued to represent them on an ongoing basis, and the courts imposed liability on the firms. In these situations, liability can be avoided only by the transmission of an unequivocal closing letter. It should also be noted that these letters can be constructed so that they have a positive component, by encouraging the client to engage the firm in ongoing representation based upon a new, agreed-upon engagement letter. The third reason for using closing letters is that they provide an opportunity to establish the arrangements regarding the retention and subsequent destruction of the client's file. Accordingly, unless the answer to questions 35 and 36 is yes, the firm should review its policies and procedures regarding the use of closing letters.

Collections

Questions 37 through 40. In many firms, the collection of outstanding accounts receivable is principally the responsibility of each billing partner. However, this arrangement is unlikely to yield uniformly successful outcomes, especially because whatever problems underlie the client's failure to make timely payment may have been known to the partner in advance. Similarly, lawyers who have an interest in continuing a relationship with a client are frequently not in a strong position when it comes to extracting payment from a reluctant client. As a way to minimize risks posed by unpaid bills and potential fee disputes, collections are best handled by administrators who are divorced from the provision of legal services to the client. Accordingly, the answers to these questions will assist the firm in determining whether it is managing the collection process in a way most likely to accomplish collection and reduce the risks that are posed by fee disputes and by uncollectible accounts receivable.

Questions 41 through 44. Although a few firms claim to have successfully prosecuted suits for fees, probably the most axiomatic risk management precept for law firms, allowing for only a very few exceptions, is never to sue a client for fees. There are two distinct reasons for this rule. First, as indicated in previous answers, fee suits almost always result in counterclaims for malpractice. Even if the applicable statute of limitations for affirmatively bringing a malpractice claim has passed, the client will almost always be permitted to claim malpractice as a setoff. Obviously, any malpractice claim will trigger the reporting obligation of the firm's insurance policy, and insurers are never happy to see fee-related malpractice claims. Second, when firms consider the actual cost of bringing litigation to collect fees (whether in terms of lawyer time that is diverted from productive work to bring the case or in terms of payment of legal fees to outside counsel), the time lost by the lawyers who were involved in the client representation in preparing the firm's response to the malpractice claim, and the likelihood that the matter will ultimately settle for a significant discount from the total sought, there is ultimately little real benefit even from a successful suit. It is thus vital that, at a minimum, firms permit litigation for fees only after the most careful review, both of the validity of the claim itself, the likelihood and potential strength of any malpractice counterclaims, and the ability of the client to pay an award even if the firm was successful. Such review needs to be made by senior management, and the billing or responsible lawyer must not have the final say in the decision that is made. Accordingly, the preferred answer to question 41 is no; but if it is yes, then the answer to question 42 should be no, and the answers to the remaining questions clearly need to be yes if the firm is to be sure of avoiding the kinds of risks just described.

ANSWER AND ANALYSIS SHEET 5

Docket (Tickler or Critical Date Reminder) and Calendar Systems Questionnaire (Page 75)

FUNCTION

This questionnaire is designed to determine what policies and procedures are actually in place and operating effectively (or otherwise) in the areas of document control, time and deadline management, and file management, from the perspective of lawyers at every level of seniority and from every practice area.

To be most useful, this answer and analysis sheet (otherwise known as the crib sheet) should not be read or reviewed until all the questionnaires have been completed by everyone who is participating in the survey process (including the firm's management and non-management groups). Then a three-step review can begin. First, each individual may consider his or her responses in the light of this crib sheet; second, the management and nonmanagement groups can meet separately and everyone within each group who completed this questionnaire can compare notes; and third, the consensus of the nonmanagement group can be shared with the firm's management. This will yield contrasting insights—what is perceived to be in place by those actually in the trenches compared to what management believes to be happening. Whether there is great congruence or significant disagreement, the responses will demonstrate for every element of the calendar and docket management process the degree to which the applicable policies are followed and procedures function, or exist but do not function adequately, or do not exist. This process is intended to lead to a consensus on the current state of the firm's policies, procedures, and controls in the areas of document control, time and deadline management, and file management. Based on this analysis, the firm can make practical and meaningful judgments about whether and which changes are required and appropriate, and in what order—consistent with the inevitable tensions between the firm's management culture and the dangers inherent in doing nothing.

For many firms, the answers yielded by these reviews will either be reassuring or will enable them to decide on and implement needed changes to their policies, systems, and procedures. For some, on the other hand, the answers yielded by these reviews may create dilemmas or the potential for internal conflict of a kind that leads these firms to conclude that outside, independent, and specialist guidance is required to arrive at strategies and tactics for implementing needed changes. In that event, help is available from a number of sources. First, many professional liability insurance brokers (and some underwriters) have staff that is knowledgeable and available to give guidance in many areas. Second, the authors of this QUIC Survey system are available to consult and provide assistance and guidance, as, no doubt, are other independent consultants.

SCOPE

This crib sheet, like its companions relating to the other QUIC Survey questionnaires, is designed to raise issues and provoke self-examination within the firm. The central purpose of the questions and the crib sheet is to help determine whether the firm has a comprehensive system and appropriate policies and procedures to ensure that calendar and deadline management operate effectively throughout the firm. Thus, the answers and analysis contained in the crib sheets are intended to perform two functions:

- explain and define the key problems and risks that the underlying questionnaire is intended to uncover in the context of a particular firm
- generally review the ethical and legal issues that may arise if the management of these issues is inadequate

The crib sheets are not intended to constitute a hornbook on the law or ethics of docket and calendar management. There are many excellent books that cover these subjects in exhaustive detail. The purpose here is to help firms determine whether they have in place systems, policies, and effective procedures to enable them to supervise their practices so that they can anticipate and control the various potential problems and issues as they arise and before they become threatening. The book offers no nostrums or guarantees; rather, it raises questions based on a Socratic model and provides general guidance on the meaning and significance of the questions. This method should enable each firm to arrive at its own comfort level (and, perhaps, the comfort of its professional liability insurers) in the management of its practice.

STRUCTURE

The crib sheet follows the numbering of the questionnaire. For each question and, where appropriate, for each subordinate part of the question, the crib sheet provides three levels of guidance. First, it reviews the significance of the question—that is, why it is being asked. Second, it discussees the broad implications of each response (yes, no, or do not know). Third, it assesses the level of importance of dealing with the particular gaps firms may have uncovered in policies or procedures.

ANSWER AND ANALYSIS

Question 1

For purposes of this questionnaire, the terms "docket" and "calendar" are interchangeable and refer to the scheduling of all future events relating to the practice of the lawyers in the firm—whether amounting to formal deadlines or not. Systems for the management of time control vary between two extremes. At one end of the spectrum are firms where calendar management consists of notes kept on loose scraps of paper and the backs of envelopes by individual lawyers, and where docket control consists of pocket diaries maintained by individual lawyers or desk diaries maintained by lawyers or by secretaries. At one firm visited by one of the authors in the not-too-distant past, calendar management was accomplished by the use of blackboards in each lawyer's office, with the managing partner overseeing the process by means of a daily walk through the office. At the other extreme are calendar systems maintained on a network computer accessible to and used by all lawyers and staff, incorporating reminders and backup reminders, with oversight by specially assigned support staff, all designed to ensure that all professional obligations pertaining to all client matters are met on a timely basis.

The key component of any adequate time-control system is that it provide two kinds of backup: first, that more than one person be responsible for monitoring each scheduled event or deadline so that one person's failure is not fatal to meeting the schedule; and second, that there be reminders before the arrival of the event or deadline to allow time for necessary preparations. Some systems, based on case management software, provide an important additional functionality: that when a given deadline is met and the appropriate activity completed, it is marked thus in the system and the next applicable deadline in the matter is automatically placed on the calendar.

No system—however sophisticated—is foolproof. After all, every system works on the GIGO principle (garbage in, garbage out), so that unless the necessary information is entered into the system, the system cannot spit it back out when required. It is for this reason that any form of personal diary or calendar that is not electronically linked to the network calendar presents a threat to the integrity and utility of centralized calendars. When lawyers are asked which they trust more, their personal diary or the network calendar, most lawyers will prefer their personal diary. Accordingly, the optimum systems require lawyers to dispense with any personal diary or calendar other than a personal digital assistant that can be linked and synchronized with the network calendar.

Evidently, at whatever point on the spectrum of sophistication any given firm lies, the policies and procedures that establish at least a minimum level of consistent calendar backup for all lawyers in the firm need to be in writing. Accordingly, if the answer to question 1 is not yes, there is cause for concern.

Questions 2 and 3

It follows from the previous answer that calendar systems can be centralized on a variety of bases, whether for the entire firm, for individual offices, or by practice group. What is important is that no lawyer be permitted to practice outside the scope of some form of calendaring system that is operated and overseen by the firm and that is more than his or her personal diary. Accordingly, the only answer to question 2 that should be cause for concern is (c). The answers to question 3 will indicate, by elimination, which practice groups are not centrally managing their dockets.

Questions 4 through 6

As indicated in the prior answers, while computerization is the most efficient way to operate calendars centrally, it is not essential. However, whatever the format in which calendars are maintained, it is preferable (but, again, not essential) that responsibility for entry be centralized rather than dispersed to individual lawyers or their secretaries. Centralization promotes expertise, whereas dispersion of the ability and obligation to answer crucial calendar and deadline events creates the risk that matters will be improperly entered or not entered at all. One of the benefits of computerization is that electronic data can be stored off-site, so if access is compromised because of a disaster, the data will still be retrievable. The same is not true, of course, when calendars are maintained only on paper, which can be irretrievably damaged or lost. It will be appropriate to assess the answers given to these questions to determine the degree of security—or risk—that exists in the firm.

Questions 7 through 9

It will be apparent from the prior answers that individual lawyers who maintain their own individual calendars present a serious risk to law firms. If the answer to question 7 is yes, there is serious cause for concern. While every lawyer is, of course, responsible for meeting deadlines, the objective for law firms in this context is to ensure that all deadlines are ascertainable even if the lawyer responsible is, for any reason, unavailable. It is for this reason that independent oversight and management of every centralized calendar system is preferable. While there are no right or wrong answers to questions 8 and 9, ultimately it is lawyers, not support staff, who get sued for malpractice if deadlines are incorrectly calculated or entered. Accordingly, while many firms use support staff, sometimes aided by computerized deadline calculation software, to perform the docket management and the docket entry function, lawyers should remain actively involved in the oversight of law firm dockets.

Question 10

As indicated in prior answers, while lawyers will frequently prefer to maintain personal calendars, this creates the ever-present risk that the data in the centralized system, which is the only one others can use to verify deadlines if the individual is inaccessible or the personal calendar lost, will be less complete and accurate. Accordingly, the preferred answer to this question should be no.

Questions 11 through 13

As indicated in prior answers, the technology is presently available to enable lawyers to maintain personal calendars electronically that automatically synchronize with central calendars. It has been shown that firms that use this technology and provide their lawyers with the appropriate tools have the greatest control over their dockets and face the least risk of missed deadlines.

Questions 14 through 17

Although these questions evidently apply most potently to litigators or firms with significant litigation practices, as well as to lawyers and firms who practice in the area of intellectual property, the calendar system should be on from the moment that each new client or matter engagement is accepted by the firm. It is prudent for there to be careful review of initial deadlines and statutes of limitations by both the lawyer responsible for the matter and by whoever is responsible for overall calendar management. It is important that the answer to question 14 be yes, that all the lawyers within the relevant practice areas can correctly identify the responsible authority at question 15, and that questions 16 and 17 also be answered yes.

Question 18

A senior partner in a prominent national law firm involved in a high-profile litigation matter recently sought to blame the paralegal "responsible" for deadline calculation and entry for the mistake that led the firm to miss a crucial filing deadline. Self-evidently, the lawyer and the law firm—not the paralegal—will ultimately be held accountable for such mistakes. Accordingly, any answer other than yes should give rise to concern.

Question 19

The lists and types of information included in the subparts are by no means exclusive. What is intended is a basic checklist for principal practice groups to demonstrate what a complete time-control system can bring to them. As previously indicated, there are two real benefits from establishing time control at this level of detail—risk management, in the avoidance of claims based on missed deadlines, and improved client service, flowing from improved practice and time management itself. In each area, therefore, the more affirmative answers, the better—plus any additional categories of information that may be valuable to your firm's practice needs. Equally, firms where substantially none of this information is available or controlled centrally should be deeply concerned at this lack of management and control.

Questions 20 through 24

These questions are intended to present additional ways in which centralized calendar management systems can operate to provide the maximum utility and efficiency within law firms. The more ways in which your firm presently provides this information, and the greater the scope of the calendaring information that is circulated, the better. If none of the information systems identified in these questions are presently in circulation at your firm, fresh thought needs to be given to calendaring and docket management.

Questions 25 and 26

Question 25 is intentionally repetitive of information sought earlier in this questionnaire. If even one lawyer answers yes, the firm is at risk of missed deadlines for the reasons previously discussed. The greater the percentage of lawyers indicated in the answer to question 26, the greater the risk facing the law firm.

Questions 27 through 29

This aspect of law practice management may be "boring" and administrative, but it is important. The file-opening procedures are discussed at length in the crib sheet for the New Client/Matter Intake Questionnaire. There are many reasons for requiring management approval before new clients or matters are accepted or opened. These questions look at the administrative element following such approval. A key element of file identification, location, and control as well as time recording and billing is a single, firmwide numbering system, even among multiple offices. Any answer other than yes to these questions ought to be a matter of concern.

Questions 30 through 33

The insurance implications of storing or holding original documents, original evidence, or other items of intrinsic value relating to client matters are often misunderstood. Original documents and other materials should be systematically catalogued and segregated, with their location very precisely recorded at all times. If such material is lost or destroyed, even if as a result of a disaster where the law firm is not in any way at fault, and a client is thereby harmed, the firm's malpractice insurance policy will probably not cover the loss. The reason is that, as the insurer will argue, the loss was not the result of an "error, act, or omission." If any insurance policy will cover the loss, it will be the firm's property coverage. But unless the firm maintains, regularly reviews, and updates a schedule of all such material, the firm may not have adequate coverage. Accordingly, it is important that the answer to questions 30, 31, and 33 be yes, and that the answer to question 32 be some relatively frequent period.

Questions 34 and 35

It is critical that the firm have a document retention and destruction policy, and that this policy be communicated to clients whose files the firm may keep after the representation ends. Both the Rules of Professional Conduct and substantive law may impose obligations on firms to maintain certain documents for a specified period of time. In addition, before destroying documents, the firm must notify clients whose files are affected and give those clients sufficient time to request return of their files in lieu of destruction. As firms move toward a paperless practice, physical document storage will likely become less of an issue. Accordingly, the answer to question 34 should be yes. Question 35, relatedly, asks whether the firm has a policy in place to close client files. The answer to this question should also be yes. Before the firm can appropriately file or dispose of documents, the firm and client must have an understanding that the representation has ended.

Questions 36 through 40

The subject of closing letters generally is more fully discussed in the crib sheet for the Client Relations Questionnaire. However, it is relevant here in connection with document and file retention and destruction policies. Firms that do have policies and procedures for the routine use of closing letters frequently include their file retention and destruction policies in these documents. Certainly, if firms are regularly using closing letters, these provide a useful vehicle for communicating this information. Accordingly, for the reasons discussed in the crib sheet for the Client Relations, Fees, Billing, and Collections Questionnaire, including the timely communication of this information, the answer to questions 37 and 38 should be yes. Questions 39 and 40 seek to determine whether this information is provided to clients in other ways, such as in initial engagement letters, if closing letters are not customarily sent.

Questions 41 through 43

It is important for all staff, including lawyers, to be reminded regularly of the final control procedures in place at the law firm. If the answer to any of these questions is no, there may be a need to reinforce training to ensure that file maintenance policies and procedures are being scrupulously followed throughout the law firm.

ANSWER AND ANALYSIS SHEET 6

Practice and Human Resource Management Questionnaire (Page 79)

FUNCTION

This questionnaire is designed to explore the nature and scope of the policies, procedures, and systems in place in the law firm for the management of both professional and support staff, including partners, management of the quality of legal services provided to clients, management of practice groups and of multiple offices, hiring practices and procedures including lateral hiring of senior lawyers and mergers with other firms, and training.

To be most useful, this answer and analysis sheet (otherwise known as the crib sheet) should not be read or reviewed until all the questionnaires have been completed by everyone who is participating in the survey process (including the firm's management and nonmanagement groups). Then a three-step review can begin. First, each individual may consider his or her responses in the light of this crib sheet; second, the management and nonmanagement groups can meet separately, and everyone within each group who completed this questionnaire can compare notes; and third, the consensus of the nonmanagement group can be shared with the firm's management. This will yield contrasting insights—what is perceived to be in place by those actually in the trenches compared to what management believes to be happening. Whether there is great congruence or significant disagreement, the responses will demonstrate for every element of the process the degree to which the applicable policies are followed and procedures function, or exist but do not function adequately, or do not exist. This process is intended to lead to a consensus on the current state of the firm's policies, procedures, and controls in the areas of human resource and practice management. Based on this analysis, the firm can make practical and meaningful judgments about whether and which changes are required and appropriate, and in what order—consistent with the inevitable tensions between the firm's management culture and the dangers inherent in doing nothing.

For many firms, the answers yielded by these reviews will either be reassuring or will enable them to decide on and implement needed changes to their policies, systems, and procedures. For some, on the other hand, the answers yielded by these reviews may create dilemmas or the potential for internal conflict of a kind that leads these firms to conclude that outside, independent, and specialist guidance is required to arrive at strategies and tactics for implementing needed changes. In that event, help is available from a number of sources. First, many professional liability insurance brokers (and some underwriters) have staff that is knowledgeable and available to give guidance in many areas. Second, the authors of this QUIC Survey system are available to consult and provide assistance and guidance, as, no doubt, are other independent consultants.

SCOPE

This crib sheet, like its companions relating to the other QUIC Survey questionnaires, is designed to raise issues and provoke self-examination within the firm. The central purpose of the questions and this crib sheet is to help determine whether the firm has a comprehensive system for managing the firm's most precious assets—its human resources at every level—and for managing the quality of legal services provided every day to the firm's clients. Thus, the answers and analysis contained in the crib sheets are intended to perform two functions:

- explain and define the key problems and risks that the underlying questionnaire is intended to uncover in the context of a particular firm
- generally review the ethical and legal issues that may arise if the management of these issues is inadequate

The crib sheets are not intended to constitute a hornbook on the law or ethics of human resource or practice management. There are many excellent books that cover these subjects in exhaustive detail. The purpose here is to help firms determine whether they have in place systems, policies, and effective procedures to enable them to supervise their practices so that they can anticipate and control the various potential problems and issues as they may arise and before they become threatening. The book offers no nostrums or guarantees; rather, it raises questions based on a Socratic model and provides general guidance on the meaning and significance of the questions. This method should enable each firm to arrive at its own comfort level (and, perhaps, the comfort of its professional liability insurers) in the management of its practice.

STRUCTURE

The crib sheet follows the numbering of the questionnaire. For each question and, where appropriate, for each subordinate part of the question, the crib sheet provides three levels of guidance. First, it reviews the significance of the question—that is, why it is being asked. Second, it discusses the broad implications of each response (yes, no, or do not know). Third, it assesses the level of importance of dealing with the particular gaps firms may have uncovered in policies or procedures.

ANSWER AND ANALYSIS

New Employee Orientation

Questions 1 and 2. The nature and scope of the initial orientation given when lawyers at every level join a law firm is enormously revealing of its culture generally and of its commitment to risk management in particular. In some firms attention is paid to newly hired first-year associates, with time spent not just on the mechanics of firm operations (computer systems, timekeeping software, availability of support staff) but also on the practice management structure of the firm, including introductions to practice group heads, mentors, and more senior associates, work assignment systems and procedures, and a review of the firm's benefits policies. Frequently, however, laterally hired associates and more senior-level laterally hired partners, after a cursory review of the operation of these systems, are introduced to the support staff with whom they will be working, shown their offices, and expected to get to work. What is missing from these descriptions is the element that ought to be at the front and center of every new lawyer's introduction to a law firm, namely, an in-depth discussion of the firm's values and priorities with particular emphasis on all the risk management topics discussed in this book—client selection policies and practices, time recording and billing practices, expectations regarding the protection of client confidences, calendaring and docket systems, and most important, an introduction to the firm's general counsel, an explanation of his or her role, and a discussion of the expectations that every lawyer will communicate with general counsel whenever any ethical problem or risk is identified. In addition, new hires at every level of seniority should be told or shown where to find the specific policies and procedures, whether in a printed manual or electronically within the firm's intranet. Unless all these issues are thoroughly covered in any formal orientation presented to all new professional hires—however senior—the firm's orientation system is inadequate.

Questions 3 and 4. The orientation given to support staff, particularly those who will have any contact with clients (including secretaries, paralegals, and receptionists), is every bit as important as the orientation provided for newly hired lawyers. There are two reasons for its importance. First, often it is the support staff with whom clients first interact when communicating with the firm. Second, it is often the support staff that is assigned the responsibility for compliance with the firm's policies and procedures of all kinds, whether completing client/matter intake forms, entering or correcting time, preparing bills, or managing calendars. Perhaps most important of all, even though obviously not subject to professional discipline, the support staff must—under the direction of the firm and its lawyers—protect client confidences and secrets. This topic alone should require a training session by general counsel or a senior lawyer. And, just as all the lawyers are trained, the support staff should be trained in the expectations of the firm, including the instruction that if they become aware of problems or issues relating to the appropriate handling of client matters or relating to the behavior of any person in the firm, however senior, they will report their concerns promptly either to their supervisor or to general counsel (who must therefore be identified and introduced to them, and whose role must be explained). Unless all these issues are thoroughly covered in a formal orientation presented to all newly hired support staff, the firm's orientation system is inadequate.

Practice Management

Question 5. Practice group management is an essential element of every law firm's risk management arsenal. There are two reasons that practice group management is so central. First, effective practice group management enables firms to ensure that every client receives the highest quality of legal services the firm is institutionally capable of providing. Second, practice group management, properly structured, enables the earliest possible identification of the problems that inevitably arise in the course of law practice, which in turn permits the firm to manage and control those situations before they become crises and, indeed, often before there are any external consequences.

When practice groups are structured for maximum effectiveness, each group is broken down into teams of eight to ten lawyers. Each team in turn consists of a vertically diverse cross section of lawyers from the practice group, from senior and experienced partners down to paralegals or those working within the same general area of expertise. These teams operate as follows:

- The teams are required to include lawyers working for multiple clients.
- Every active matter is assigned to a team immediately on file opening.
- An individual team member is responsible for oversight of each matter.
- Teams are required to meet at regular intervals.
- The status of all active matters is required to be reviewed periodically at team meetings.

Structured and operating in this manner, team practice can provide enormous benefits for clients, for all the lawyers involved, and for the firm.

For Clients

- They always receive the best practices of the firm, not just of an individual lawyer.
- There is continuity of service if individual lawyers are absent, incapacitated, or otherwise committed.
- Each engagement is completed within the shortest feasible time.

- They receive continuous on-the-job training.
- Workloads are allocated fairly.
- Morale is improved by the collegial approach to practice.
- The quality of life is significantly enhanced—no one is indispensable, and everyone supports one another when personal free time is needed.

FOR THE FIRM

- Clients become property of the firm, not of individual partners.
- There is improved integration of lateral partners and merged practice areas.
- Errors are identified and prevented or remediated before harm is done to clients.
- Profitability is enhanced by increased efficiencies, speedier delivery of product to clients, and happier clients.

Question 6. To determine whether practice group management has been effectively and comprehensively established, every lawyer must be assigned to a practice group. Any answer other than yes to this question means that a practice group system is not yet fully implemented in the firm.

Question 7. As discussed in the answer to question 5, matters should be assigned to practice groups and then to teams. In that way, all clients of the firm can be assured that each matter will receive the best practices of the firm as a whole rather than of an individual lawyer.

Questions 8 and 9. At the furthest extreme from team practice is solo practice. Within law firms, solo practice occurs for one of two reasons: either the firm has only one lawyer in a given area of expertise, or an individual refuses or is unable to practice collegially. These questions seek to identify whether there are any solo practitioners because of their expertise and if so, the particular practice areas within the firm. At a minimum, law firms should consider adopting the Noah's Ark principle, namely, at least two experienced lawyers in any practice area.

Questions 10 through 14. These questions are designed to establish the degree to which individual matters are handled on a daily basis by solo lawyers. Even if a law firm is not ready or is not large enough to implement team practice as described in question 5, every matter should be regularly reviewed by a lawyer other than the lawyer normally responsible for the matter. This alternative to practice management, while it does not have all the benefits of team practice, at least provides some level of assurance that clients are receiving an appropriate level and quality of service, and that problems are being identified and remediated, on a timely basis. If the answers to these questions demonstrate that solo practice in the firm is widespread, the firm may conclude that the practice group structure needs further development. It should not be an acceptable answer that having a second pair of eyes on every matter is uneconomic. If the economics do not justify this minimal level of oversight, then the firm needs to review its client selection criteria and its client intake management. If only a few matters would be uneconomic when subjected to this oversight, the firm should consider this kind of regular review as a management necessity regardless of the economics.

Question 15. This question is designed to ferret out solo practitioners, who often appear in law firms as a result of lateral hiring or as a result of decisions to provide a "service" practice area that is outside the scope of the firm's normal expertise. These pockets of unsupervised practice pose a rise to firms because when a "solo" practitioner makes a mistake, it will only become known to the firm when the suit for malpractice is commenced, and there is no way to identify or remediate it on a timely basis. On the other hand, where matters are handled by several lawyers, there is a much greater likelihood that mistakes will be caught and rectified, and harm to the clients avoided altogether, or at least minimized.

Question 16. The benefits of assigning work initially to teams rather than individuals are described at question 5.

Question 17. Even if firms have concluded that practice oversight can be accomplished adequately using the second-pair-of-eyes approach, there are obvious risks if one of the lawyers working on or overseeing each matter is not a partner. Accordingly, if the answer to this question is not yes, there is cause for concern.

Questions 18 and 19. One way that firms sometimes approach the practice oversight challenge is through the use of mentoring programs. This question is designed to determine whether there is a formal structure for supervising the work of all associates. Unless the firm has already moved to team practice or has instituted matter-by-matter oversight, any answer other than yes to question 18 or no to question 19 should be of concern.

Questions 20 through 25. These questions seek to establish how effectively the firm disseminates its risk management policies and procedures, beginning with the moment at which lawyers and staff at all levels are hired and continuing thereafter. Effective risk management in a law firm requires that every lawyer and staff person in the firm understands the obligation to report any problem or issue that may constitute a threat or claim against the firm, its lawyers, or its clients. These questions and their subparts seek to identify the degree to which the firm has expressed these obligations in written policies and whether these policies have been disseminated throughout the firm. Only if these policies are known and understood can the firm hope to identify and control problems at an early stage rather than merely reacting to a crisis. Alcoholism, along with drug dependency or any other form of addictive behavior, affects the individual concerned as well as the firm and its clients. It is important for firms to have in place policies and systems for both identifying and dealing with lawyers suffering from any such problem at the earliest possible moment. These questions are intended to determine whether the firm has appropriate policies and systems in place, and whether the staff at every level has been properly educated. Unless it is clear from the answers to all these questions and their subparts that substantially all the firm's lawyers are fully familiar with the expectations of the firm as to how they should respond to any of these situations, it is important that the firm review its risk management oversight and the adequacy of training in this area. For further discussion on these topics, please refer to the crib sheet relating to the Risk Management Oversight Questionnaire.

Opinion Letters

Questions 26 through 29. In addition to formal opinion letters prepared for clients, an opinion letter can be any letter intended or known to be relied on by a third party who is not a client of the firm. Opinion letters include letters responding to requests from auditors, letters involving tax advice—and for this purpose, letters to clients are included in the definition—and letters that constitute Sarbanes-Oxley reports. Regardless of the general or specific category within which an opinion letter falls, opinion letters generally constitute a significant area of risk for law firms. Indeed, the recent spate of claims and settlements regarding the issuance of tax opinions should make the scale and severity of this risk apparent to all. Key to managing risk in this area is the existence and enforcement of policies and procedures ensuring independent review, within the firm, before lawyers with client or matter responsibility can issue opinion letters. However resistant lawyers may be to oversight of their practices, the fiduciary obligation among lawyers within firms entitles the firm to require individual lawyers to submit documents that will bind the firm for such review, in the interest of protecting the entity and all its individual members—as well as the intended recipients of the opinion letter. Accordingly, these questions explore the procedures and policies in place to control the issuance of opinion letters. If issuance of opinion letters is a regular element in the course of a firm's practice, any answer other than yes should be a cause for serious concern about the management of this aspect of the practice.

Supervision

Questions 30 through 32. Basic human resource management requires regular and formal reviews of all employees regardless of a firm's size. Any answer other than yes ought to prompt a reconsideration by the management of the firm's employee relationships.

Question 33. To be effective, either for the evaluation itself or for appropriate communication with the person being evaluated, the review process must be structured. To give confidence in the process, this requires some level of formality, of written checklists of issues to be covered, a record of the process, and responses. The record should relate to all elements of the process described in the subparts, particularly 33(f) through 33(j). A vital element of risk management is identifying problems in the firm at an early stage; it is often the associates who are confronted with or are aware of these issues in the first instance, and it is important to use that knowledge constructively, to catch problems before they ripen into crises. Accordingly, this aspect of associate reviews should be taken very seriously, and the firm's commitment to reporting of and constructive response to problems should be stressed. If the answer to any of these questions is not yes, an in-depth review of the firm's human resources policies and procedures should be undertaken.

Question 34. The health of the firm's senior lawyers should be a matter of concern for two reasons: regard for the welfare of each individual and the provision of consistent and adequate service to clients. Accordingly, to the extent consistent with applicable laws governing human resource issues, answers other than yes should give rise to at least some discussion within the firm as to whether adequate attention is being paid to the subject.

Question 35. Lawyer departures can sometimes occur in circumstances that are fraught with risk, including appropriate treatment of clients as well as disputes involving what is owed in either direction. Accordingly, it is important that firms have written policies and procedures that clearly express the rights of both the firm and of the departing lawyers, whether contained in the firm's partnership or shareholder agreement or in other written form. Accordingly, any answer other than yes should result in a review of the firm's policies and practices in this area, and, if necessary, the drafting or revision of the appropriate documents.

Due Diligence Regarding Lateral Hires

Questions 36 through 38. The dangers of inadequate due diligence in the hiring of lawyers at a senior level or in law firm or practice mergers should be all too apparent, but many firms do not do for themselves what they would insist on for their corporate clients. Unless risk management policies, procedures, and controls are uniformly in effect throughout the firm—including in satellite offices, wherever located, and in every practice area—they cannot have the intended protective effect. There are multiple instances of awards and settlements in the millions of dollars because of lateral hiring decisions that turn out to have introduced Trojan horses into law firms. In addition to verifying all the elements listed in the subparts to question 37, it is important, both as part of the due diligence process and for the compatibility of practice philosophies, to determine whether a potential lateral hire individually—or merger candidates collectively—come from cultures that accept the same level of risk management as in your firm. Any answer other than yes to any of the elements of these questions should be a serious cause for concern regarding how your firm reaches hiring or merger decisions.

Questions 39 and 40. Even if the answer to question 38(l) is yes, it has been the experience of many firms that the information provided—in good faith—before a lateral hire or merger relating to conflicts of interest is incomplete. Accordingly, it is important that as soon as the lateral hire or merging law firm arrives, a complete review be conducted of each new client and new matter to be opened, just as the firm would do if these were new clients or new matters being introduced in the ordinary course of business. Failure to do so can result in the loss of both valued existing and anticipated new clients. Accordingly, the answer ought to be yes to every element of these questions; to the extent that this has not been past practice, this area should be carefully reviewed.

Question 41. The significance of this question will be apparent from a review of the answers to questions 5 through 19. Any answer other than yes ought to be a source of significant concern.

Professional Development

Questions 42 through 49. Even apart from the fact that failing to meet CLE requirements can in some states result in lawyers' suspension from practice, CLE is an important component of effective risk management. Firms that conduct CLE internally are probably the most focused on providing targeted programs meaningful and useful to their practices. But even if firms are not providing CLE internally, it is perfectly feasible to oversee participation by the lawyers in appropriate, relevant, and high-quality programs delivered by outside providers. These questions are intended to establish whether there is appropriate oversight of compliance with CLE requirements in states that have mandatory CLE, as well as what steps firms are taking to supervise the substantive training of their lawyers. Question 49 is intended to highlight the importance of legal ethics CLE in a firm's overall risk management program.

Question 50. In addition to CLE, it is good practice for firms to periodically educate their attorneys about internal policies and procedures. Compliance is likely to be greater if attorneys are aware of and attuned to such policies (and understand that management is committed to enforcing them). Similarly, firms could benefit from training their lawyers on risk management and proper handling of potential malpractice claims.

Succession Planning

Questions 51 through 54. It is vital that law firms consider succession planning, not only to maximize the likelihood that they will retain the business of retiring lawyers but also to protect against mistakes resulting from an aging lawyer's decline in competence. Confronting a colleague about potential cognitive decline can be very uncomfortable, but avoiding the situation or covering for the affected attorney will only make the situation worse. Questions 51 and 52 are intended to help firms evaluate whether they are, at the very least, aware of these issues. Questions 53 and 54 address a related but different issue: whether the firm's organization encourages attorneys to transition their clients to more junior lawyers in an orderly way before retirement. Firm compensation structures that reward attorneys for originations can encourage hoarding, which ultimately harms the firm as a whole. Firms should consider adopting hybrid systems that reward attorneys for thoughtful succession planning.

ANSWER AND ANALYSIS SHEET 7

Trust Accounts and Financial Controls Questionnaire (Page 85)

FUNCTION

This questionnaire is designed to explore the nature and scope of the policies, procedures, and systems in place in the law firm for the management of funds and property held by the law firm for clients and third parties, in client trust and escrow accounts, including compliance with applicable ethics rules.

To be most useful, this answer and analysis sheet (otherwise known as the crib sheet) should not be read or reviewed until all the questionnaires have been completed by everyone who is participating in the survey process (including the firm's management and nonmanagement group). Then a three-step review can begin. First, each individual may consider his or her responses in the light of this crib sheet; second, the management and nonmanagement groups can meet separately, and everyone within each group who completed this questionnaire can compare notes; and third, the consensus of the nonmanagement group can be shared with the firm's management. This will yield contrasting insights—what is perceived to be in place by those actually in the trenches compared to what management believes to be happening. Whether there is great congruence or significant disagreement, the responses will demonstrate for every aspect of client and third-party fund and asset management the degree to which the applicable policies are followed and procedures function, or exist but do not function adequately, or do not exist. This process is intended to lead to a consensus on the current state of the firm's policies, procedures, and controls when the firm holds funds or property for clients or third parties. Based on this analysis, the firm can make practical and meaningful judgments about whether and which changes are required and appropriate to protect the firm from liability claims and to ensure compliance with all applicable ethics rules.

For many firms, the answers yielded by these reviews will either be reassuring or will enable them to decide on and implement needed changes to their policies, systems, and procedures. For some, on the other hand, the answers yielded by these reviews may create dilemmas or the potential for internal conflict of a kind that leads these firms to conclude that outside, independent, and specialist guidance is required to arrive at strategies and tactics for implementing needed changes. In that event, help is available from a number of sources. First, many professional liability insurance brokers (and some underwriters) have staff that is knowledgeable and available to give guidance in many areas. Second, the authors of this QUIC Survey system are available to consult and provide assistance and guidance, as, no doubt, are other independent consultants.

SCOPE

This crib sheet, like its companions relating to the other QUIC Survey questionnaires, is designed to raise issues and provoke self-examination within the firm. The central purpose of the questions and the crib sheet is to help determine whether the firm has a comprehensive system for managing property of clients and third parties in the firm's custody. Thus, the answers and analysis contained in the crib sheets are intended to perform two functions:

- explain and define the key problems and risks that the underlying questionnaire is intended to uncover in the context of a particular firm
- generally review the ethical and legal issues that may arise if the management of these issues is inadequate

The crib sheets are not intended to constitute a hornbook on the law or ethics of the handling of client and third parties' property. There are many excellent books that cover this subject in exhaustive detail. The purpose here is to help firms determine whether they have in place systems, policies, and effective procedures to enable them to supervise these elements of law firm structure so that they can anticipate and control the various potential problems and issues as they may arise and before they become threatening. The book offers no nostrums or guarantees; rather, it raises questions based on a Socratic model and provides general guidance on the meaning and significance of the questions. This method should enable each firm to arrive at its own comfort level (and, perhaps, the comfort of its professional liability insurers) in the management of its practice.

STRUCTURE

The crib sheet follows the numbering of the questionnaire. For each question and, where appropriate, for each subordinate part of the question, the crib sheet provides three levels of guidance. First, it reviews the significance of the question—that is, why it is being asked. Second, it discusses the broad implications of each response (yes, no, or do not know). Third, it assesses the level of importance of dealing with the particular gaps firms may have uncovered in policies or procedures.

ANSWER AND ANALYSIS

Question 1

This question seeks to determine whether the firm maintains the appropriate accounts, as required by applicable ethical rules, when the firm receives funds or assets from clients or third parties. Unless the firm never receives such funds, it is vitally important that every person completing the questionnaire answer yes. Any other response necessarily demonstrates that there are people in the firm who are unaware either that the appropriate accounts exist or that the appropriate controls are in place. Any such responses would indicate the immediate need to review every aspect of the firm's policies and procedures and to disseminate these policies throughout the firm.

In addition, the Rules of Professional Conduct for each state contain specific directions regarding what types of financial institutions may be used to house escrow or trust accounts and where these banks must be located. It is thus vital for firms to know what the rules are in every state where it has an office. Firms should also monitor these rules periodically to account for any changes.

Question 2

Again, unless every person responding correctly identifies the individual responsible for the management of trust, client, or escrow accounts, there is a need to review every aspect of the firm's policies and procedures for handling client or third-party funds and to disseminate these policies throughout the firm.

Questions 3 through 5

Although most jurisdictions have no rule prohibiting firms from delegating signatory authority of a client or other trusts or escrow accounts to nonlawyers, it is lawyers (and, in a few states, firms) that are subject to professional discipline including, not infrequently, disbarment for failing to adequately manage these accounts. Although there is no right or wrong answer to question 3, it is advisable that the signatories on these accounts be lawyers, even in states that do not have a specific ethical rule to that effect. Similarly, the ethics rules of most states provide that every lawyer (or at least partner/shareholder) in a firm is responsible for the proper management of these accounts. Accordingly, it is never an excuse to say that another lawyer was responsible for managing the accounts, and numerous disciplinary decisions have held that "innocent" lawyers are as culpable and responsible as those actually managing the accounts. Prudence therefore suggests that two signatures should be required for all withdrawals from trust, escrow, or client accounts to ensure strict compliance at all times with applicable rules.

Questions 6 through 8

The maxim "trust, but verify" applies with special strength in the management of all law firm bank accounts, but especially to trust, client, and escrow accounts. Accordingly, unless regular internal audits are performed, there is always a risk that these accounts are not being managed appropriately and that funds have gone or will go astray. Any answer to question 6 other than yes should not be acceptable. Similarly, the applicable policies should be written and easily accessible (as well as regularly disseminated) to every lawyer in the firm.

Questions 9 through 12

The authors are aware of a number of situations where law firms have taken on lateral hires or have merged with other firms without taking appropriate steps to identify and take over the management and control of client and escrow funds and accounts from these lawyers, and significant disciplinary and liability issues resulted from that failure. It is therefore an essential part of the due diligence process when a lateral joins the firm, or when firms merge, to review all the files and all the bank accounts formerly under the control of the newly arriving lawyer or lawyers to ensure both that they have been properly maintained in conformity with all applicable rules and that they are promptly transferred to the control of the firm. Accordingly, any answers to these questions that do not confirm the existence and enforcement of policies and procedures that actively oversee the identification and transfer of responsibility for client and third-party assets to the firm from newly arriving lateral hires or most practices should be a cause for serious concern.

Questions 13 through 17

Holding Funds for Clients. Model Rule 1.15 sets forth the many requirements for lawyers who hold client funds in escrow. The authors believe that it is best for firms to refrain from holding such funds. Safeguarding client monies can lead to potential disputes that require the firm to withdraw from the representation as well as to claims for malpractice or breach of fiduciary duty. Law firms are not banks; they are not set up to manage funds. Moreover, holding such funds requires administrative time and effort for no reward. Firms may have an interest in accepting settlement funds on behalf of clients, in part to ensure that their fees are paid, but they should be aware that this practice is not without risk. For example, lienholders may file claims against the firm for failing to honor liens. In the vast majority of instances, the risks outweigh the benefits of holding client funds.

Holding Funds for Nonclients. Apart from the ethics rules governing the management of client funds, significant risks arise when law firms hold funds for third parties that are not clients. First, unless there is a written escrow agreement, it is all too easy for a dispute to arise over the proper application of these funds as between the firm, its client, and the third party in question. Such a conflict may prevent the firm from continuing to represent its client. Second, unless the escrow agreement explicitly deals with the question, there is the additional risk that the third party may assert that it is also a client of the firm, which would necessarily create exposure to malpractice claims as well as unintended conflicts of interest. In some cases, firms that have handled funds from third parties have been exposed to claims that the firms actively aided and abetted fraud or some other improper conduct. The acceptance of funds from third parties that are not clients may also be subject to significant regulatory control, such as under the laws relating to terrorism, or, if the funds come from abroad, under the laws governing money laundering. For all these reasons, firms should not act as escrow agent for third parties that are not clients, and therefore the answer to question 14 be no. If the firm does choose to serve as escrow agent, funds should never be accepted from any third party that is not a current client of the firm other than in accordance with clear and written policies. Even then, such funds should be accepted only after the execution of a written escrow agreement in an approved form. Such approved forms should expressly provide that the third party is not a client of the firm and does not become one by virtue of the execution of the agreement, and that, in the event of a dispute, the only duty of the firm shall be to deposit the funds or assets with the court. Accordingly, if the answer to question 14 is yes, an answer to any of questions 15 through 17 other than yes should be a source of very serious concern and should result in a prompt review of the practices in place regarding these issues and the development and uniform enforcement of appropriate policies, procedures, and controls.

Question 18

If the firm ever handles client or third-party assets, it is highly recommended that the answer to this question be yes. The authors are aware of all too many instances where trusted employees, even partners, absconded with funds, leaving others to make good the loss, in a few cases to the tune of millions of dollars. The cost of these kinds of policies is not great, and in the event of fraud or theft, the benefit and support will be significant.

Question 19

Unless the firm makes and publishes clear policies regarding expense reimbursement, attorneys can very easily take advantage. The authors are aware of multiple examples of attorney abuse of expense reimbursement that caused not only financial losses but significant public relations issues for their firms. If a client is to be charged for meals, travel, or other work-related expenses, that client should be made aware of and agree to the types of reimbursable expenses up front. Failing to take this step can lead to unnecessary strife between the firm and its client. Similarly, the firm should be transparent about what it is willing to reimburse to prevent after-the-fact disputes with attorneys and staff members. Some firms choose to provide firm credit cards to attorneys to monitor spending; others permit or require attorneys to pay expenses out of pocket and seek reimbursement. Firm credit cards are riskier unless the firm religiously adheres to review of actual receipts to determine appropriateness. Whatever method the firm chooses, it will ultimately save the firm money and time by having a clear up-front policy.

Questions 20, 24, and 25

In addition to setting out what expenses are reimbursable, the firm should require documentation of actual receipts before providing reimbursement. The firm should also have staff that does not simply rubber stamp requests but thoroughly reviews the documentation provided and ensures that all necessary receipts are produced. This process should be fully published to the firm's attorneys. This will prevent the firm from losing money on improper charges and discourage attorneys from attempting to abuse the system. This is particularly important when the expense at issue will be charged to a client. Any answer other than yes to question 24 is a cause for concern.

Questions 21 through 23

Requiring prior approval for significant expenses is prudent firm policy. Even if a particular type of request, such as airfare, is generally reimbursable, the firm may be unpleasantly surprised by the amount of a particular expense. To operate efficiently, the firm should have a system in place to quickly process expense and reimbursement requests. And, while it may go without saying, expense and reimbursement policies are of limited use if they are not monitored for compliance and enforced as written.

Questions 26 and 27

A firm's outside auditors can be a helpful resource for more than year-end financial statements. They may also help firms determine whether their internal financial controls are effective. Random review of bills sent to clients is another useful measure of compliance with the firm's billing and reimbursement policies.

Question 28

If anyone in the firm becomes aware of a potentially noncompliant bill that person should feel comfortable raising the issue with someone in a position to address the problem. This generally means having a designated person to deal with such issues and making it clear who that person is and that he or she is approachable. As with client intake issues, this person should be someone other than the lawyer who initially generated or approved the bill.

Questions 29 and 30

Firms should have their annual financial statements audited by an outside auditor to catch any errors that might have been made by internal bookkeepers. In addition, given the high percentage of disciplinary matters resulting from escrow violations (both intentional and unintentional), it is a good practice to have the firm's accountants periodically review the controls in place on firm bank accounts, specifically client trust accounts.

Question 31

It is becoming increasingly common for clients, particularly large institutional clients, to provide their lawyers with outside counsel guidelines. These guidelines may differ from typical firm practice with respect to assignment of personnel, billing, and expense reimbursement. Firms are at risk of being bound to such guidelines by individual partners and then misplacing or failing to comply with the guidelines. It is critical at the intake stage for the firm to know whether such guidelines exist and equally critical when it comes to billing to monitor compliance with those guidelines.

ANSWER AND ANALYSIS SHEET 8

Technology and Data Security Systems Questionnaire (Page 87)

FUNCTION

This questionnaire is designed to explore the nature and scope of the policies, procedures, and systems in place in the law firm for data security and the use of technology. The rapid changes in technological tools, coupled with the risk of data breaches from both internal and external sources, make these topics exceptionally important for law firms to address.

To be most useful, this answer and analysis sheet (otherwise known as the crib sheet) should not be read or reviewed until all of the questionnaires have been completed by everyone who is participating in the survey process (including the firm's management and nonmanagement group). Then a three-step review can begin. First, each individual may consider his or her responses in the light of this crib sheet; second, the management and nonmanagement groups can meet separately, and everyone within each group who completed this questionnaire can compare notes; and third, the consensus of the nonmanagement group can be shared with the firm's management. This will yield contrasting insights—what is perceived to be in place by those actually in the trenches compared to what management believes to be happening. Whether there is great congruence or significant disagreement, the responses will demonstrate the degree to which the applicable policies are followed and procedures function, or exist but do not function adequately, or do not exist. This process is intended to lead to a consensus on the current state of the firm's policies, procedures, and controls with respect to data security.

For many firms, the answers yielded by these reviews will either be reassuring or will enable those firms to decide on and implement needed changes to their policies, systems, and procedures. For some, on the other hand, the answers yielded by these reviews may create dilemmas or the potential for internal conflict of a kind that leads these firms to conclude that outside, independent, and specialist guidance is required to arrive at strategies and tactics for implementing needed changes. In that event, help is available from a number of sources. First, many professional liability insurance brokers (and some underwriters) have staff that is knowledgeable and available to give guidance in many areas. Second, the authors of this QUIC Survey system are available to consult and provide assistance and guidance, as, no doubt, are other independent consultants.

SCOPE

This crib sheet, like its companions relating to the other QUIC Survey questionnaires, is designed to raise issues and provoke self-examination within the firm. The central purpose of the questions and the crib sheet is to help determine whether the firm has a comprehensive system for managing data and the use of technology. Thus, the answers and analysis contained in the crib sheets are intended to perform two functions:

- explain and define the key problems and risks that the underlying questionnaire is intended to uncover in the context of a particular firm
- generally review the ethical and legal issues that may arise if the management of these issues is inadequate

The crib sheets are not intended to constitute a hornbook on the law or ethics of law firm data security. The purpose here is to help firms to determine whether they have in place systems, policies, and effective procedures to enable them internally to supervise these elements of law firm structure so that they can anticipate and control the various potential problems and issues as they arise and before they become threatening. The book offers no nostrums or guarantees; rather, it raises questions based on a Socratic model and provides general guidance on the meaning and significance of the questions. This method should enable each firm to arrive at its own comfort level (and, perhaps, the comfort of its professional liability insurers) in the management of its practice.

STRUCTURE

The crib sheet follows the numbering of the questionnaire. For each question and, where appropriate, for each subordinate part of the question, the crib sheet provides three levels of guidance. First, it reviews the significance of the question—that is, why it is being asked. Second, it discusses the broad implications of each response (yes, no, or do not know). Third, it assesses the level of importance of dealing with the particular gaps firms may have uncovered in policies or procedures.

ANSWER AND ANALYSIS

Question 1

Similar to the general counsel, a designated technology security officer can serve as a lightning rod to process and repair potential security risks. It is imperative that this person be a senior executive in the firm, with the authority to make necessary decisions and take swift action. Having an IT director, while important, is *not* the same as a technology security officer. It is also vital that attorneys and support staff know who the technology security officer is and feel comfortable approaching him or her with their observations.

Questions 2 through 4

The most fundamental obligation of every lawyer and law firm is to preserve client confidences. Today, that obligation can be fulfilled only if law firms rigorously protect their electronic data from unauthorized access. Regulatory regimes, such as the Health Insurance Portability and Accountability Act, place additional obligations on law firms to keep private information safe from disclosure. Thus, if the answer to question 2 or 4 is no, the firm should review its systems or undertake the appropriate evaluation—and maintain a timetable of periodic testing and evaluation for the future. Similarly, if a recent evaluation has demonstrated or suggested flaws, resources should promptly be allocated to correct them.

Questions 5 through 7

Written policies serve a dual function: they ensure that the writers of the policies are addressing all the issues that need to be addressed, and they are easily disseminated to everyone in the firm who needs to be aware of them. Particularly for complicated issues such as technology and data security, the importance of written policies cannot be overemphasized. Technology changes rapidly, and lawyers have an ethical obligation to stay abreast of those developments. The best—and perhaps only—way to do that is to continually reevaluate the technologies that are available and the implications of their use by the firm. The authors recommend annual training of lawyers and support staff both as a reminder of the basic principles of data security (such as proper use of e-mail) and a vehicle for introducing new information caused by changing technology (such as social media).

Questions 8 through 14

These questions are designed to determine if the firm has the necessary basic protections in place to avoid the most common technological failures: virus-based destruction of software and data, theft or destruction through hacking from the Internet, and inadvertent disclosure of client confidential information. If the answer to any of the subparts of question 8 or to questions 9 through 14 is no, then the firm urgently needs to reevaluate its basic security protections.

Questions 15 and 16

It is permissible for law firms to outsource these functions, but the law firm cannot delegate its obligation to preserve client confidences. Accordingly, the firm is required to assure itself that providers of outsourced services use the same protections for the law firm's data as the law firm would itself and that these providers are contractually bound to preserve client confidential information. See also response to questions 22 through 25 regarding cloud computing.

Question 17

Most law firms, like other businesses, have suffered some interruption of computer operations, whether through hardware or software failures or as a result of external attacks. Law firms must have a protocol to be followed in the event of a data breach and must monitor compliance with the protocol. For example, if an attorney loses a portable device, the attorney must report the loss to the IT department immediately, and the IT staff must have the capability of remotely wiping the device. The risk of disclosure of confidential information in that circumstance is inversely proportional to the speed with which the firm learns of and can remedy the mistake. For interruptions that do not cause loss of data but create the inability to function, what is important is how efficient the firm's support staff is in bringing the systems back online.

Questions 18 and 19

If a firm has all its important data and software operating systems backed up and stored off-site, it can mount a recovery of its operations in the event of a security breach causing damage or loss. A negative answer to either of these questions should be remedied immediately.

Questions 20 and 21

Current estimates are that more than 60 percent of all documents and communications into and out of law firms are now electronic, and that sooner or later law practice will be 100 percent "paperless." But most law firms still have some paper documents. To the greatest extent possible, law firms need to be able to access both kinds of material. If the answer to question 20 is not yes, the firm should determine which documents that are not stored electronically need to be scanned and backed up.

Questions 22 through 25

Cloud computing, or the use of remote information storage accessible via the Internet, provides many benefits for firms, particularly smaller firms looking to cut down on the costs associated with traditional data storage. It also presents new challenges to maintaining electronic data security. Before contracting with any cloud storage vendor, firms must ensure that the remote point is secure and that the means of transmission of information is secure, either through encryption or other methods.

Non-Technology-Related Disaster Recovery Planning Questionnaire (Page 89)

FUNCTION

This questionnaire is designed to explore the nature and scope of the firm's existing preparations, policies, and procedures for responding to and dealing with disasters—from power outages to destruction of the firm's premises (from whatever cause)—that disrupt the firm's ability to conduct its practice. Since each firm's needs will vary, the questionnaire and this Answer and Analysis Sheet (otherwise known as the crib sheet) were developed as a self-assessment tool and guide to be considered during the business continuity planning process. The focus of these questions is to review the components of an effective plan and to compare it to the firm's existing procedures for disaster recovery. While the questionnaire and this crib sheet seek to combine best practices for business continuity planning in the law firm environment, they do not replace a firm's individual responsibility to customize its own business recovery plan. In addition to including consideration of the firm's insurance coverage as part of the planning process, at many firms the process of business recovery planning is itself considered a form of "insurance," with the planning process being the "premium" payment that is willingly paid to minimize the consequences of disasters.

To be most useful, this answer and analysis sheet (otherwise known as the crib sheet) should not be read or reviewed until all the questionnaires have been completed by everyone who is participating in the survey process (including the firm's management and nonmanagement groups). Then a three-step review can begin. First, each individual may consider his or her responses in the light of this crib sheet; second, the management and nonmanagement groups can meet separately, and everyone within each group who completed this questionnaire can compare notes; and third, the consensus of the nonmanagement group can be shared with the firm's management. This will yield contrasting insights—what disaster recovery plan is perceived to be in place by those actually in the trenches compared to what management believes to be its disaster recovery plan. Whether there is great congruence or significant disagreement, the responses will demonstrate for every element of the

155

disaster recovery planning process the degree to which the applicable policies are known, or exist but are not widely understood, or do not exist. This process is intended to lead to a consensus on the current state of the firm's disaster recovery planning and preparedness. Based on this analysis, the firm can make practical and meaningful judgments about whether and which changes are required and appropriate to enable the firm to continue providing an appropriate level of service to clients, and to operate its business, in the event of a disaster.

For many firms, the answers yielded by these reviews will either be reassuring or will enable those firms to decide on and implement needed changes to their disaster recovery planning. For some, on the other hand, the answers yielded by these reviews may create dilemmas or the potential for internal conflict of a kind that leads these firms to conclude that outside, independent, and specialist guidance is required to arrive at strategies and tactics for implementing needed changes. In that event, help is available from a number of sources. First, many professional liability insurance brokers (and some underwriters) have staff that is knowledgeable and available to give guidance in many areas. Second, the authors of this QUIC Survey system are available to consult and provide assistance and guidance, as, no doubt, are other independent consultants.

SCOPE

This crib sheet, like its companions relating to the other QUIC Survey questionnaires, is designed to raise issues and provoke self-examination within the firm. The central purpose of the questions and the crib sheet is to help determine whether the firm has a comprehensive disaster recovery plan. Thus, the answers and analysis contained in the crib sheets are intended to perform two functions:

- explain and define the key problems and risks that the underlying questionnaire is intended to uncover in the context of a particular firm
- generally review the ethical, legal, and practical issues that may arise if the management of these issues is inadequate

The crib sheets are not intended to constitute a hornbook on what level of business recovery planning is necessary or appropriate for every law firm. There are many excellent books that cover this subject in exhaustive detail.[1] Rather, the purpose is to help firms determine whether they have in place systems, policies, and effective procedures to enable them to respond appropriately, effectively, and expeditiously if disaster should occur. The book offers no nostrums or guarantees; rather, it raises questions based on a Socratic model and provides general guidance on the meaning and significance of the questions. This method should enable each firm to arrive at its own comfort level (and, perhaps, the comfort of its professional liability insurers) in the management of its practice.

STRUCTURE

The crib sheet follows the numbering of the questionnaire. For each question and, where appropriate, for each subordinate part of the question, the crib sheet provides three levels of guidance. First, it reviews the significance of the question—that is, why it is being asked. Second, it discusses the broad implications of each response (yes, no, or do not know). Third, it assesses the level of importance of dealing with the particular gaps firms may have uncovered in policies or procedures.

ANSWER AND ANALYSIS

Impact Analysis

Question 1. Has management ever considered what would happen if, suddenly and with no warning, access to the firm's offices (or any office in a multi-office firm) became impossible? It does not have to be as dramatic as the World Trade Center bombing or the flooding of the Chicago river that rendered blocks of downtown buildings inoperative and inaccessible. Rather, it could be a fire in an adjacent space, or it could be a partial disaster that makes it impossible for firm personnel to get to work or to function if they do arrive—for example, an extended telephone or power outage in the firm's building. *What would happen?* The first step in business recovery planning is to prepare a study of how your firm would—or could—function *tomorrow* if no express plans had been made to deal with various levels of disaster, from totally disabling ones to partial disruptions. If the answer to this question is no, your firm would do well to consider preparing such a study—soon.

Question 2. An essential element of such a study is the establishment of priorities. What functions are most important—internally, and to provide continuity of service to clients—and what are luxuries, or otherwise unessential, that can be dispensed with in a pinch? And, of equal importance, what are the time frames within which essential services and functions would have to be reestablished, regardless of the severity of the occurrence causing the problem? Again, if the answer to this question is no, it is time to deal with these issues.

Question 3. A business recovery plan has three key elements:

- the *actions* to be taken
- the *resources* to be used
- the *procedures* to be followed before, during, and after a disaster that renders part or all of the firm's business functions unavailable

An effective plan is critical to limiting loss and liability and may provide the following benefits:

- mitigate risk of catastrophic loss
- ensure orderly and rapid recovery

- provide a cost-effective balance of protective measures with insurance coverage
- ensure compliance with regulatory requirements (e.g., safeguarding of client assets)
- reduce costs of insurance coverage

An effective plan uses the following steps to develop methods for conducting business in a variety of disaster scenarios:

- Identify critical firm processes and recovery time frames. The firm should prioritize the functions that are necessary to do business; management should consider how much time it can afford to take to recover these functions or processes and the impact the recovery time will have on the firm.
- Define the firm's minimum requirements and an action plan to safeguard these processes.
- Select workable alternatives that are cost-effective and limit firm exposure. The firm should examine the cost of the plan components against the potential damage to the firm—and its potential liability—in the long term if the business is interrupted and no recovery plan were in effect.
- Prepare documented plans for recovery and business continuity. Formalize the plan and incorporate it into the policies of the firm.
- Test the plan and train firm members and employees. This includes the initial testing as well as regular plan maintenance.

Question 4. Obviously, there are all kinds of potential disasters, leading to different levels of disruption. The appropriate reaction and the recovery response, as well as the time scale for the restoration of full activity and functioning, will vary accordingly. It is important, in preparing the plan, to provide for these different levels of response. The appropriate reaction to a complete loss of power—which may last less than a day—or to the complete crash of a computer system will be less than to a fire that guts the office and requires a long-term, complete rebuilding or relocation of the firm's physical space. In the middle of the spectrum would be an event that leaves the office intact but inaccessible for weeks and requires intermediate substitution of all services without any long-term reconstruction. Unless the firm's existing plan is sufficient to enable the firm to check each of the subparts of question 4, the plan is likely to require additional development to avoid overreaction to minor or limited disasters.

Plan Preparation and Maintenance

Questions 5 and 6. A key element of every plan is to identify and train appropriate personnel to aid in the recovery process. Preassigned roles can include a roster of other personnel to be notified when the plan goes into effect, on the model of emergency call-ups by the Israeli army, as well as the more managerial functions involved in getting the emergency systems up and running. Training of everyone involved, like testing of the plan, should not be a onetime occurrence. If a crisis occurs, it is important that the plan be familiar, and people's roles well known and understood, or time will be lost when it is most important to reestablish the firm's operations.

Question 7. A plan—even a well-conceived one—that exists only in the head of the office manager when a disaster occurs is as useless as no plan at all. If the answer to this question is no, designate appropriate individuals to the team without delay.

Questions 8 and 9. Even a subtle change in firm procedures—a change in computer equipment, or significant software, for instance—can render existing plans obsolete as it relates to those functions. Unless the answer to both questions is yes, a review or test should be conducted immediately and a timetable drawn up for future reviews and tests. It is not necessary to close the office or firm to stage an effective test. It can be done in phases or by functions. Tests should involve more active participation from those with a role in making the plan work effectively but should also be performed in such a way as to familiarize the entire staff, professional and support, with the main logistical elements. Tests can be held periodically, for instance, to confirm that everyone knows the site and telephone number of the premises to be used if the firm's offices become inaccessible. More frequently, the system for backing up the computer data and storing it off-site can be checked. If there has been no testing, the plan is unlikely to work smoothly a disaster occurs.

Questions 10 and 11. The answer to both questions should be yes, to include *everyone* in the firm. All employees should know ahead of time what their role is and where they are supposed to go—including to stay away entirely, if that is the plan—once formally notified that the plan is in effect. This will minimize time wasted—when it is the most precious, during a crisis—explaining what people are supposed to do.

Questions 12 and 13. An essential ingredient of any business recovery plan is where the firm will operate when one of its offices is inaccessible. Obviously, no firm will duplicate its entire facility—that is why a plan is necessary. Rather, the plan must include the selection of some location, with some facilities, where the firm's operations can be organized. The firm might make an arrangement with businesses established to provide such services, or it might strike twinning-type agreements with other professionals in which each firm shares its facilities with the other in the event of a disaster that forces one party from its premises (subject to ensuring that client confidentiality will not be compromised). Organization of the recovery process will go much more smoothly if everyone knows ahead of time where the firm will be based and managed during the crisis. If the answer to these questions is no, your firm's plan is almost certainly inadequate.

Question 14. If the emergency facilities selected do not have all the equipment that will be needed to operate the firm during the recovery process, it is important that the plan at least clearly identify and list the firm's requirements, including relevant suppliers. A negative answer to this question means that time will be lost remedying these deficits when the arrangements could already be under way to fill the list if it already existed. In addition, if the disaster involves more than your own firm, there may be competition for scarce materials and the failure to have in place the appropriate list and contact information may result in significant delay in obtaining necessary items.

Questions 15 through 17. A key priority in the recovery process is reestablishing links with the rest of the world, chiefly through telephone and Internet access. How these needs are to be met will depend in large measure on the nature of the facilities selected and on the nature of the firm's existing systems. It is crucial, however, to know ahead of time how this will be handled—and to confirm that these services will be available immediately when the plan is put into effect. If the answer to question 15 is no, this gap should be plugged promptly. If the plan does not make arrangements—assuming these are possible—to have telephone calls automatically rerouted as soon as the plan is put into effect, then by definition the telephone arrangements will involve a new number during the emergency. If possible, this number should be acquired in advance and included in all copies and versions of the plan. This will greatly speed the reestablishment of other firm functions and services.

Questions 18 through 22. A corollary to communicating the firm's temporary arrangements is to provide information needed concerning those to be contacted. Since this information might normally be accessed by computer, the information should also be printed out—and updated—at regular intervals and disseminated to everyone so that it is available for immediate use as soon as the plan is put into effect. All information necessary to reestablish contact with those on the list—even if the information is obtainable online, in case the disaster precludes online access to those who need it—should be provided. Precisely because this is a time of crisis, planning should allow for failures. Accordingly, redundancy is an important goal, and every piece of information that is required by the plan to be available at the firm's offices should be available to everyone at their homes. The answer to all these questions should therefore be yes.

Support Functions

Question 23. It is not enough for the lawyers and their immediate support staff to know how and where they are expected to function during the recovery process; all the essential support functions within the law firm must also be operating. Accordingly, it is just as important that the plan deal with how other services—IT support, time recording, billing, accounting, payroll, and so forth—will function during the recovery process. Furthermore, since the plan may require people to perform tasks during this period that are different from and possibly in addition to their normal responsibilities, some functions may have to be carried out by temporary help. In that event, the firm should at least identify a reliable source for such outside help, if not make actual provision to contract for its help if the plan is ever put into effect. Accordingly, the answer to this question should be yes.

Questions 24 and 25. It will be the support staff as much as the lawyers who keep the firm functioning during the recovery from a disaster. For them to do so efficiently, they should be represented on the recovery team in whatever way is appropriate to get the firm up and running after the plan is put into effect. A negative answer to either of these questions indicates that insufficient attention is being paid to the support roles in recovering from a disaster.

Questions 26 through 29. Whatever systems are used to store firm and client documents, both hard copy and electronic data, the ability to re-create those systems will require knowing what they are. If the firm does not already maintain an effective document management system for all documents generated in the firm's practice, the preparation of the business recovery plan will demonstrate a clear reason for undertaking a program to develop such a system, not to mention the benefits of efficiency this program will yield. A negative answer to any of these questions should prompt serious consideration of this topic.

Question 30. If your firm relies on outside services for any of your operations, it will be important to a smooth recovery to ensure that they are also part of the plan and know what is expected of them if the plan is ever put into effect. In that event, the answer to this question should be yes.

Insurance

Questions 31 through 33. Unless the law firm can check off every subsection of question 31, the firm should immediately contact its insurance broker to obtain an appropriate level of any missing elements of insurance coverage. Similarly, the amount of coverage and the appropriate limits should be reviewed at least annually; if the answer to questions 32 or 33 indicates less frequent review, a discussion should be held immediately with the firm's insurance broker and a timetable established for regular reviews in the future.

NOTE

1. *See generally* GARY A. MUNNEKE & ANTHONY E. DAVIS, THE ESSENTIAL FORMBOOK: COMPREHENSIVE MANAGEMENT TOOLS FOR LAWYERS, VOL. 4, PART I, DISASTER PLANNING AND RECOVERY (ABA Law Practice Division, 2004).

INDEX